The
Wedding
at
Nether Powers

By Peter Redgrove

The Collector and Other Poems
Routledge & Kegan Paul

The Nature of Cold Weather and Other Poems
Routledge & Kegan Paul

At The White Monument and Other Poems
Routledge & Kegan Paul

The Force and Other Poems
Routledge & Kegan Paul

Work in Progress
(Poems 1969)

The Hermaphrodite Album
(with Penelope Shuttle)

Dr Faust's Sea-Spiral Spirit and Other Poems
Routledge & Kegan Paul

Sons of My Skin: Redgrove's Selected Poems 1954-1974
Routledge & Kegan Paul

In the Country of the Skin
Routledge & Kegan Paul

The Terrors of Dr Treviles
(with Penelope Shuttle)
Routledge & Kegan Paul

The Glass Cottage: A Nautical Romance
(with Penelope Shuttle)
Routledge & Kegan Paul

From Every Chink of the Ark and Other New Poems
Routledge & Kegan Paul

The God of Glass
Routledge & Kegan Paul

The
Weddings
at
Nether Powers
and other new poems

PETER REDGROVE

ROUTLEDGE & KEGAN PAUL
London, Boston and Henley

First published in 1979
by Routledge & Kegan Paul Ltd
39 Store Street, London WC1E 7DD,
Broadway House, Newtown Road,
Henley-on-Thames, Oxon RG9 1EN
and 9 Park Street,
Boston, Mass. 02108, USA
Set in Baskerville 11/12 pt
and printed in Great Britain by
Caledonian Graphics

British Library Cataloguing in Publication Data

Redgrove, Peter
The weddings at Nether Powers, and other new poems.
I. Title
821'.9'14   PR6035.E267W/   79-40201

ISBN 0 7100 0255 6

Contents

Acknowledgments

Grateful acknowledgments are due to the following magazines and anthologies in which certain of the poems first appeared: *Agenda*; *Ambit*; *The American Scholar*; *Bananas*; *Bananas Anthology*; *Biala*; *Delta*; *Encounter*; *Folio*; *Forum*; *Gallery*; *Hard Edges*; *Helix*; *Kudos*; *The Listener*; *London Magazine*; *Meridian*; *New Poems 1977-78* (P.E.N.); *New Poetry 3* (Arts Council); *New Poetry 4*; *New Statesman*; *Other Poetry*; *Outposts*; *Pacific Quarterly*; *Pearl*; *Pick*; *Poetry Australia*; *Poetry Book Society Christmas Supplement 1978*; *Poetry Dimension 6*; *Poetry Review*; *Poetry South-East*; *The Scotsman*; *South-West Review*; *Thames Poetry*; *The Times Literary Supplement*.

Acknowledgments are also due to the BBC who first broadcast certain poems in a programme 'Cornwall's Redgrove'; and to Words Press (*Ten Poems*) and The Priapus Press (*Happiness and Other Poems*) for their booklets. 'A Roadside Feast' won the Prudence Farmer Award of the *New Statesman* for 1977.

THE VISIBLE BABY

A large transparent baby like a skeleton in a red tree,
Like a little skeleton in the rootlet-pattern;
He is not of glass, this baby, his flesh is see-through,
Otherwise he is quite the same as any other baby.

I can see the white caterpillar of his milk looping through
  him,
I can see the pearl-bubble of his wind and stroke it out of
  him,
I can see his little lungs breathing like pink parks of trees,
I can see his little brain in its glass case like a budding rose;

There are his teeth in his transparent gums like a budding
  hawthorn twig,
His eyes like open poppies follow the light,
His tongue is like a crest of his thumping blood,
His heart like two squirrels one scarlet, one purple
Mating in the canopy of a blood-tree;

His spine like a necklace, all silvery-strung with cartilages,
His handbones like a working-party of white insects,
His nerves like a tree of ice with sunlight shooting through it,

What a closed book bound in wrinkled illustrations his father
  is to him!

RICH JABEZ DOG

Jabez Dog felt very rich. Smells among the gorse
And strawberries, there was a smell
Of honey everywhere, he felt at last
He was one of three persons, Father, Son and Dog,
And as he trotted into the wood he felt Apostles near,
He looked among the trees with his nose for those Apostles,
Then he looked at the trees, they were the Apostles.

The approach of an Apostle is like the approach of an oak;
The approach of an acorn through the earth
Is like the approach of an Apostle: but these were female,
Female oaks, like bearded Apostles with tits:
Jabez felt his piss inhibited: flowers without yellow pollen!
It was unnatural, he wanted a sunlit oak,
The yellow light attending on the sunny pollen
Through a day of expressive balsams of the trees
Emaned in changing rainbow-odours through the day.
This was unnatural: a grove of bitch-oaks!

But then a new smell like a spirit walked through
All the trees at once, it was less a smell itself
Than a doorway to one unimagined yet, like the negative
Of crushed coconut, which is gorse, or like a golden door
Of honey slowly opening, and the opening opening:

Virgin Jabez gathered himself, and leapt through.

THE WOOD

The wood ticking like a water-clock,
The drops gliding on slant twigs like funicular tears;
They hewed great tree slices, piled them up, forgot.
The wood contains a city of tables and chairs,

2

A countryside of doors, a continent of windowframes;
The wood is a secluded library full of shelves
And on the shelves softening books
And through the waterdrops like glistening spectacles
The vision of unborn librarians pores, of carpenters takes
 measure.
I open this book with an axe,
The grain pours within like a slice of a waterfall;

I slice open an acorn: down the corridors of power
Oak-lined parliaments approach, and votes approach
Like forests of people shedding green rain.

HORSES OF THE DUST

Ants like slim horses trotting in their valleys,
Galloping with hollow hooves over the grey cinders,
Caught in a shower darkening in splodges, they
Are faster than the rain, they see it coming
Like the hulls of glass liners.

                                        Ants full of grass,
Their lips pincing grass-tufts, their tight plates
Panelled over juicy flow, the ant-milk
Oozing from their leg-joints;

                                  and parched desert ants
Like lacquered skeletons with ruminant jaws.

They live in cities which are called *The Queens.*
Each room in that city is called *A Queen.*
Sometimes their Goddesses are carved within tree-trunks
Others are flat Goddesses, spreading under stones.

Lift one, look into the Goddess's side, watch her blood
In its rooms, each blood-speck a skeleton,
Or a thin horse, exquisitely formed.

3

OR WAS THAT WHEN I WAS GRASS

I was putting a bandage of cobweb on the sudden cut
In the pain the fly told me what the web was like
The spider's face with its rows of diamond studs
And my skin crackling as the pincers drove in
That crackling pain went all over me
I knew I would never grow well again, my shell crazed,
And the acid came from the jaws and began to turn me liquid
And I felt a terrible pressure all over with the suction
And I was drawn up through the tusks into that face.
Then I woke up as though I were in a distillery
Humming with energy, retorts of horn and transparent tubes
Buzzing with juices, but I was at rest
Sealed like wine in crystal vases, and I looked down myself
With my eyeskin which was the whole egg, and I felt
The wine condense and become smoky and studded with rows
Of the eyes through which I saw that the mother watched
Benevolently from the roof of the factory which was herself
And my father whom she had eaten was with me too
And we were many flies also contributing to the personality
Of the eight-legged workshop, and I began to remember the
    man
I had fed on as a maggot or was that when I was grass
Or the snail slying from my shell crackled on the thrush's
    anvil?
And whenever my eyes closed or my shell crackled in pain,
It was as though I stepped out of black winged habits.

MY FATHER'S KINGDOMS

The lovely shimmering skins of water
Swooping between the lions
The gown of water of Trafalgar Square,

4

The hollow brides of water:
These belonged to my father;

And the policemen pacing it in their deep clothes,
Their silver switchgear on their Queen's helmets
They belonged to my father, said 'Good-day'

Saluting like the thunderous city.
All the clothes of the city-men, the umbrellas,
The sponge-bag trousers and the stiff white collars

Belonged to my father, the starched points,
The studs, the charged tie wedged in the points,
The sparkling shoes trotting down Threadneedle Street
Like city serge bright-sewing

These belonged to my father, and at the City's centre
God sat like a dome and with wide eyes
And broad wings and a smart tolerable beard
Jesus swam through St Paul's ceiling, said 'Good-day'

Saluting like the thunderous city
Which belonged to my father

The BBC's sparkling hair
Of lines of electricity that reached into our homes,
The voices that were correct from London

Belonged to my father
The trains belonged and the clocks obeyed the trains
And Selfridges and Father Xmas and Richmond Park
Belonged to my father, and his father gave it to him.

Even the bombs that fell on London
Belonged, he let a few in.

UNDRESSING FOOD

His first meal after the resurrection,
Everything around him ready to open, to give up its dead.
He stares at the pears amazed, he expects them to fall
Sliced, and to step forth powers
Tiny, bright, and naked as pips,

As he himself miraculously stepped forth
Out of an opening in the hill's side,
Out of the upside-down tree of the grave,
Up among the gravestones all the same
Like a game of grey chess won by pawns.
The repressive pieces do not stir.

He pauses among them expecting descendents,
His tunnel black at his feet,
But the first sleeper wakes first
And steps down into the road
A winding thousand miles of emptiness

And in stairs overhead the thundercloud
Made of black stepped galleries, beehive
With its swarming resurrected rain,
Gives out its single note, its one bright sting;

Will a human voice descend the black stairs? assuredly
Great powers tread them; or is this road of pears
Where the skins smell as though he were drinking them
All there is? It would be enough,
Before the others step forth he hopes for a second death.
He drinks the pearskin odour,
He breaks the fruit as though undressing it.

DRUNK ON THE MOON

The bowling down the hill of blazing wheels,
At the time of solstice, mother of grasses:
That grass slope was a great individual with
Personal feelings and her armpit hair
Down to her elbows. The moon is covered
With swaying lawns of grass, the green moon,

Rippling like a round river.
She is mother and refuge of the ghosts
So the women smear themselves with the white clay
Becoming like ghosts and moonlight

And, to celebrate the grass, their wigs meet
And mingle in their grass skirts and grass sandals, each
      woman
Wears a rippling outside, like exterior cunt.

I have seen the vanishing of the veiled man in his own shadow,
The empty ghost-muslin settle softly on the rippling grass,

I have seen the well of the beautiful dance fill to the brim,
Overflow in clear streams through the rippling grass;

I have seen forsaken Eleusis celebrating itself
As the light bursts like water from the birth-cone
Saying 'Awareness in the womb', and I have seen
The headless man take three tottering steps, which is a torso
Whose head is situated beyond death, in some rippling place,

And the grass wigs led me, meaning awareness in the earth.

IN THE CHARTS

As he cut his thirteenth cake
My brother wished for hairy legs;
At this a small portion
Of the acoustic church that encloses us
Appeared in the minute gap
Of our loudspeaker
Switched on by father;

The great programme arriving
Shuddering from crest to crest
Crept through our equipment
In diminished rhythmic measures;
Ours was a softspeaker,
No need to magnify the intolerable giants
Striding through surfy ethers!

Who took up in their hands
His wish for hairy legs,
Passed it round the world
Back to Broadcasting House

Which has radios that tune in on us
Just a little, since we all want so much,

And played a tune that caused the hair to spring and my
    brother
Danced to it with the girls, and fifty million others.

BORN

Born with a little cap of slime, his caul,
The midwife washed him, and the skin floated off,
She fished it out like a paper-bag,

Shut it in the dictionary, P-Z. Later
She peeled it off the page and folded it in a locket
She gave him on her death-bed, in the scent
Of coal-tar soap; even her death
Smelt like nurses; and when he wore it

For his own death he tried to rip the locket away:
It must be evil! for he wanted to rest
Closing his eyes but they were transparent
Like a caul and he saw the room unchanged
Except for his nurse who had arrived as his eyes shut.
She stretched out her arms as though he were drowning
But when he opened his eyes there was only his wife
Drowsing on a chair, but shutting them more people had
    arrived
With straining arms and faces about his bed,

And then the soap-smelling midwife bent and pulled at his
    face
And took a squalling red thing out of his head
With a little cap of slime, and he was awake
Among the grown-up people, his head being sponged
And the corpse floating off like tough paper in the bath.

A ROADSIDE FEAST

He slaps the hedgehog off the road
He chivvies it off with scraping prongs
He pins it alive on metal points
The blood catches the starlight
He says you must watch for fleas and not touch the vermin
He prods it down in the bank of clay
He stirs it round until it is an earth ball
Taking a twig he scrapes this off
Into the heart of the fire where it glows
And sizzles like a speeding cannonball

9

A high-pitched cry of juice from a blowhole;
With his trowel he dibbles it out on a stone
Taps it and cracks it, the clay shards-off
He pulls these with scalding fingers
A roasting smell pays attention, we lean forward,
Like a six-inch pig the naked food
Glorious with grease. He waves us off
Bake your own hedge-pig, he says.
I pick up a shard, daggered with long pins.

FRAME

I

I polish my ring, the motors glide by,
The centipede nourishes himself in his toilet skirting
With mahogany pincers on housebreaking woodlice;
He runs like a chest with polished drawers
Opening and shutting; he runs with a face
Made of furniture, like a case of chisels,
Like abattoir sorting-bays full of hooks,
He runs like a beaded frame of some deserted photograph.

II

I place a photograph of my son there, it does not fit.
Of my wife, of my aunt, ah, no, that is not it.
I place the General there and that's the one
Even to the complicated straps of his Sam Browne
And the great switchgear-badge mounted on his cap,
His binoculars in his hand, staring up from a map;
My cousin the young policeman with the ash-blond hair,
The hat of black-and-white checks, belongs there,
The black mirror of his hat-peak, his cindery hair
Within the chisels of the centipede, boxy wriggler:

Like boxes on elastic, the police-cars
Scattering and hooting after juicy burglars.

MR SPEAKER, MS WHISPER

A fountain parted in the middle and combed back,
How it draws the MP's out on to the terrace with its whisper
To listen to the white noise of the water
That contains all speeches and includes all Hansard
In its white noise of page-riffling, each page hissing
With the knowledge in it, then the sun strikes
And the rainbow beams from the fountain, the Members
Applaud scatteredly, take this image
Back into the Chamber, where presides
A bald man with the false hair of a woman,
Splitting hairs, not sunshine into hanging rainbows.

STEEL QUEEN

Medal ribbons writing on his chest,
The Queen peers to inspect them;
A Queen's language of spectra;
The rainbows of oily battlefields.
His hand goes up as if on wires, salutes:
The ships drift past; the working boats
Work past, black against bright water,
Rigged with jib, foresail, mainsail, mizzen,
Like Chinese letters full-sailing,
Signifying: 'I bring stores', or
'I fear the Manacles but am stalwart',
Or, steel letter: 'I am the Queen's Ship;
You must hold your peace.'

WEATHER BEGINS HERE
(*Cornwall*)

I throw a quick bight of halliard round a cleat,
My lantern carves the darkness like a knife.
Much of the weather of England is born on Goonhilly Down,
It is dispensed from there in concentrated form
That England dilutes *ad lib*. Sometimes syrup-of-thunder
With streaks of lightning in it, or solid sunshine
Hewn in convenient lengths for up-country;
The Coastguard retails weather in damp job-lots
Over the radio; rain cut in measured bundles
Like rushes, downpour sheaves; the coastguard's dials
In his glass cottage perched on the granite cliff
Sample the gales, his pictured windcharts
Catalogue his wares, he has

Armies of travelling graves to send over the sea;
He can ripen the harvest, his forecasts trample the wheat.

INITIALS OF THE DEAD

The grandaddies carved their initials on these trees.
You enter the beechwood as you'd enter a pipe-organ
Of neat harmonic ranks, and on the pillars
Entwined initials like a hall of fame,
A cenotaph of living wood. The letters
Grew with the trees, we tip-toe past
Tombstones a hundred feet tall, and now the breeze
Works the pipes and pedals and cannot find the tune,

And great alphabets bend towards us, softly moaning.

12

THE BARGE-RIDERS

A string of barges whose names are effaced,
Heavy riders of the brown tide,
Horse-coloured boats, wood rich as fruit-cake.
The people within are people apart,
Whose homes glide on the river.

You with your home clutching its bedrock,
Do you wish for an Oxford door, a Falmouth door?
The cities glide past on their business,
The lamps swing from the roof.
We live in rhythm measured by long waters.

It takes us a mile of brown glittering canal
To rein in for the lock-gates.

THE ONLY WHITE THING

Beside the cottage, the river-gates
Complex as the jaws of an insect;
In the oven, the crusty dome rises.
The weather coils like a seashell
Made of thunderclouds and enormous voices.
She carves mountains out of the bread,
We lower our heads to say grace;
The thunder utters; in a dark room
By the inky lock, bread is the only white thing.

13

OLD MASONRY

The mason who made the stone wall is now the wall,
The damp mason with his smell of stone
Within the wall with his pick on his shoulder
And his stone sandwiches and his sandpaper trousers
And his stone shirt and his cap like rough stone flowers.
It is no use trying to chip him out of his courses,
Out of his work like some cave drawing or stalagmite,
It is no use trying to break him out of this wall
By shattering him into his pieces, he would fall in his stones.
Better by far to enjoy his work with the mosses
In the sunlight with the streaming pattern of mason's
    shadows.

NUNS, WRINKLED

The fear of the Lord is clear, and flowing for ever.
It is the holy water that makes them so perfect and so
    wrinkled.
As though a cathedral of shady oaks should arrange its grain,
They waddle in black towards us arranging those wrinkles.

Because God scares them and they are so kindly,
Their faces are never at rest, are tattooed with restlessness;
The fear of the nuns is deep and clear,
And wrinkled for ever.

Their faces are given to the Lord, who wrinkles them,
Who has folded them up for his pocket and hands them back
Like used handkerchiefs.

He wipes his bloody face
With nun's thoughts, with nun's faces.

14

This woman in prayer
Like bed-sheets ironed with death-diamonds.

Their skins are wrinkled as the Bible is seamed with versicles,
And their eyes blank as holy water; I watch a sister
Walk up to the holy abbess and with two fingers into the
    vesicles
Dip in her eyes and cross herself with moist patches.

MAN OF THE OTHER CHURCH

I

This cow is a church, its flesh and blood
Is a congregation, its bones the stone pillars,
The tombs ruminate the useful grass of the past,
And I am the Parson preaching to the cow.
My gestures pass in front of her eyes,
She is used to me, and her calves
Like bishops emerge from an oily consecration.

II

I climbed up into the tree for my pulpit,
I preached to the grass from a height, it sighed,
I talked to the tree's shadow, which is its ghost
That travels through the grove; then I saw
That the birds had dark ghosts, like all the grass!

III

I would not break your arm, my brother,
O tree, I would not break your twig.
I hear the genius of the oak lamenting,
No one will take its verses to dictation,
It scribbles in all its fibres, its crown

15

Is a breathy hush with whispers, it creaks
Like a ship. By chewing its gum
I have formed a blood-brotherhood, and I have purchased a
    dog
For if this brother of mine is ever cut down
(The axe-strokes bright as primrose-banks)
I will direct his ghost into my dog
To prophesy before my hearth. When *he* dies
In his sleep, in his running-dream,

I shall plant him in the forest and I shall have placed
Acorns in his mouth and in his haunch. His ghost
Will bark through all the trees. Was my pulpit a dog?
This oak that I ride was a horse, I am cantering
In its green saddle. Does the ghost
Of the church pulpit enter Parson's feet
And, ascending, inspire his brotherhood with oaks?
Am I a succession, and not just one Parson
Preaching to oak pews, preaching to uncut pulpits?

Trees walk over the earth, where do our children's souls
Come from, but from the forests, I hear them crying
In the boughs. What dignity the people have,
The dignity of trees, now I can preach to them,
My flock rooted in the pasture, tossing their acorned heads.

GODHEADGEAR

I

I was about five when I saw God's face in a dream,
He was a man-face floating alone high in the sky
Topped with a black beret, his serious pale face
Bitten into by a beret, his watchful face
Brooding over the pane of the flowing sea,
A tight hat slanted on his head like a commando,
A beret jammed on his head like a Frenchman,

Like a child of the Thirties who hates his hat,
In the dress uniform of a Chelsea Artist
Hovering over the sea like his pleated smock:
In a sea-green smock, he is frowning into his belly.

II

Is God a Frenchman? Is he a small child
Ashamed in a hat his parents laugh at?
The beret in the Fifties was a hospital style
After leucotomy, to keep the shaved head warm,
The hat-rim clear of the taped skull-cuts
Where the bistoury had sliced off voltage transmissions
Of 'I will slaughter my kids', from
'How soft their breathing.' *I feel cured!*
He said, with most of his brain.
A surgery popular then; on the upgrade again.

III

Is half God's brain missing, is this why he wears
The black badge of leucotomy, of the baby-killer?
Is the pale brow gristle, for serenity,
Like Melville's cartilage-cliff, that white whale-brow?

IV

Later God showed me another dream. Like a judge
There he floats above the tides, in his black cap;
He snatches it off and the lovely hair tumbles,
The sheer raven in stepways of perfume!
God, snatch off your clumsy biretta,
Pluck off for ever that syndicate hat,
Whale of Ages, eschew your bitter fedora,
Defer in your own presence, uncover,

Pull off your head of hair that shadow of the Mafia.
If you came in disguise, doff it now;
If you are pregnant with your tides, we shall wait them out;
If you are in your bloody courses, we shall not say *child-killer.*

17

SALMON-MURDER

Salmon-murder reddens the valley stream; I saw it pulsing
Down beside the town and I thought it iron-stain
But for the silver bodies swirling down, fish
Bruised like the moon. At the head of the beck
The Minister's Pool, and the little Force
Only tall as a twelve-year girl, and white in spate,
And the great tweeded men with their clubs, thigh deep in
      the pool
Like baseball players swiping the brave fish as they leap
Catching them flying and with their blows killing them
Reddening the valley stream with salmon-murder
As though the harvest bled, and leapt from the scythe.

ONE TIME

Her dress rushed and glistened as she went
She carried a green handkerchief
We walked through the first act of a great thunderstorm,
We sheltered in the silent ovens.
The clay had been built so deep and thick in the pottery
That no thunder reached us there, only the violet flicker
Through the doorways; the floor soft dry sand.
Now when I make love the memory of that time
Rises through my skin, her skin
Rushes and glistens as it goes, and the black thunderstorm
Deep in the silent ovens, lightens.

18

GOD HEADS

God kisses every child all the time
All at once, he says;
He sees clearly the bones of the statues.

In the hubbub of the swallows
On their skidding flight at evening
To catch the dew on their wings
To greet the white boulder-moon rising,
He regards the boulders
Scattered over the hills
Like unused statues,

Like figures that tried to walk
And walked but were stone still
That strolling cracked to pieces.

There was a head though
That learnt to roll
You can see its track

To where it invisibly sits
Kissing all its children at once,
A track as though a city had slid;

It sits where it sits
Feasting all its own saints,
Spreading their tables:
The rock-eating saints

These are statues, he said
Of incipient saints,
Crumbs over the green hillside.
They are patient,
Stony, like heads made all of teeth,
Incubating lips,

Incubating tongues,
Everything incubates

He said, I wonder where that other great head is,
Watching over his shoulder as the moon rises.

THE UNIVERSAL FACES

The aquarium-girl riding the jetting faucet.
Luminous tattoos nuzzle the glass,
The fishes are beacons and feathering buoys,
Bug-eyed faces loom seriously

Like the captain who has swollen
To the size of his liner without losing purpose.
This friend bred a fish that had the same
Solemn-humorous look with the down-turned mouth
And long nose as his partner, so when death arrived

His lover's face on wings
Fluttered in all the aquariums. He has sold

The patent on the breed, which was hardy
And haunted the aquariums from Tokyo to Sandusky,

Glass panes rippling with his lover's living photos!
Then a gourmet's teeth greeted the flaky ghost-flesh:

Suddenly the world was full with bouillabaisse of him!

And they escaped, sea-bred, were trawled,
Were popular with chips, fried in batter,

Everyone digesting and becoming his lover! All the heads
Littering the canneries and buried for fertiliser,
The beaches of England thick with his lover's shoals.

He threw himself off Dover, the universal faces ate him.

UNCLE MONEY

There were no bones in the tomb, only strings of cash,
Pierced coins tied together on thongs,
What I had taken for a skull was a soft bag
Of coins and the shadows the coins indented from within
Resembled the contemplation of a bone-face;
I opened it. 'Is this uncle, then? under the flesh,
Coins of the realm?' The black girl with the crowbar
Opened the dark-lantern so I could see the bones of gold:
'That is a gift-horse,' she said, 'spend uncle and be glad.'

PLATALOW'S BUNG

She is a memorial to the idea of the bungalow;
Plato's Bungalow, the bungalow with the name-plate
For the postman, 'Plato'. I asked him, is that a name
Or are the people there called 'Plato'. 'Oh yes,' he said,
'That is the bungalow of the Plato family: Jim Plato,
Shirley Plato, and little Lettice Plato, and they call their
     dog . . .'
'Don't tell me,' I said, 'they call it "Socrates" ',
'No, as a matter of fact, it bit me the other day,
So I know its name, the brute is called "Diana", it
Drew blood.' 'Thank you, postman, so that I shall know
You again, you are Mr — Actaeon?' 'No, Lord
Love you, Sir! not at all, my name's Ed; Ed, Sir,
Ed Imion, and my mother was Greek.'

VILLAGE ON THE SOUND

As the sky-smith beat out from bloody clouds
A bronze moon it began ringing like a gong;
'Those are the sounds,' the Ironsmith told me
As he plunged the glowing crescent horseshoe
Into hissing clouds of horsehoof steam,
'Of the village during the day, played back by our great hills.
Listen!' I heard the patter of children's feet,
And children's laughter returning from the dark schoolhouse.
He said: 'The sounds of life pouring into them
On sunlit days, pour out again at night
In one fast wave; the dog can hear
Every detail . . .' his dog stood by the forge
Pointing, '. . . and with practice you can catch
A faint after-wave of former years; when anyone
Has raised his voice it is recorded.' I heard
The dead people quarrelling out of the green slopes,
Now inky-black in moonlight; 'It is a crystal
Of the hills,' he says, 'vibrates in tune
As the crystals of the moon pass overhead;
Our history rises from those hills
Like a steam of sound; listen again!
It's time for the battle': I heard
The violent people hacking at each other. 'This shame,'
He said, 'the crystals take note of, they do not hear
The quieter sounds of love and people-making.'
'I think they do,' I replied, 'look at the dog':
Still pointing, in the utter silence.

THE BLIND SIGHT

Under shock-haired Cloud Jeremy,
A hollow globe of birds astonished by thunder!
Black Jeremy foams across the land on his white rain-skirts.

The bird-bomb explodes in squarks, they are usually better
    prepared.
Jeremy speaks in a Gravel Telepath voice, down to our bones
Which ring like gongs. We wanted to take a dry walk.
You can do this with the map-rod if you know braille.
To feel that rod is to take a journey, it is carved
As far as the quarry, and you can see with fingers
The smashed conch stone and the millions of scree
But not new-born Cloud Alice, who barely grazes the sun.
With it you can enter Round Bottom Church
And finger the tiny font among the immense tombs,
Which give this message: read me in the Church.
For that, true blindness is requisite: I see a tomb
On which small figures enact a carved funeral;
My blind friend kneels, and runs his fingers over the tomb.
His face lights up, he laughs, his fingers are busy still,
His face is alight, he is as though sighted; I say
'What is it, Jack?' He says, 'If only you could see!'

CLIENTS AND PATIENCE

The holly is full of white patients.
The holly is a waiting-room of thorns and fretwork
The white sheet webs of spiders gown them
In the dusty storeys of hollies
Blanched by the road-dust,
The whitish chalky legs of the spiders
Patient that not only dust will disturb them:
It is a school of tailors with tailors' patience,

They will run up a sheer white suit for any fly-by-night,
They will do it silently while the customer struggles,
They will poise their scissors over the white satin chest and
    stain it.

THE SHRINKING CLOCK

The pug-nosed bluebottle butts my window
Buzzing like a watch that shrinks the day
Into a hundredth of itself: now it walks
The white cross-beams and enters the sunny stage,
The light strikes rainbow sparks from its black waxes,
It is covered with oily spectra, like a black motorcyclist
It stands and preens in the hot sun-patch;
It is not clockwork: it is not filth;
It is a spark of the sun that knows the sun
And clothes itself with the sun; its eggs
Are sculptured urns of the sun, like sallow
Grains of wheat; it is a winged lion of the sun
Roaring, high-pitched and very fast roaring.

BAD MANOR IN DECLINE

People in Turner's style glaring at a poppy of clouds,
The strong sunset over the sea in about eighteen forty;

Sheep grazing Salisbury Plain like disciplined clouds
Tasting a green salad at an earthen table;

A bedroom with beige bed-curtains, and a great cobweb
Like chiffon from bedpost to lacquer wardrobe;

They have been spider-speaking fibrous words:
These webs record their relationship since the old man died.

There is almost as much said in this upper room
As in the library with the blacklace carving and pier-glasses,

The tales in half-calf waiting for dustless evenings.
I sit with my quill in the portrait and read a cobweb.

24

All the doors are ajar in the enfiladed rooms,
They bang twice a day, in the dawn wind, and at sunset.

They are a veil of openings spun by loquacious furniture.
In the picture of an interior in a plain Flemish style

What inventories quill-written by the painted poet at the
    console table,
What instructions and plans for the ticker-tape spider

Tapping and spinning beyond frames and portrait-painting
    mirrors.
Watch! all the canvasses, all the mirrors, are sliding aside,

And the spiders troop out, their arms full of soft gossamers.

FROG-LEAP PLOPS

Frog-leap plops into the sandy water,
The water, the jouncing spring, its bubbles,
The fresh and skinny frog that dances
Upright in the spring,
The little clean legs, the clean satiny mechanisms,
The body of clean cushions and levers, lips and lenses,
Shimmering mucus and clean silky muslins;

The green cock-frog decays, still dancing
In the sandy spring while his generations
Of flickering black tadpoles surround him like black fire
He feeds them

Ah the water is a clean organ again
Dancing an upright pencil-thin skeleton.

25

Frogs are the cleanliness of water,
Not mere streamlined water in fishy capsules,
But water dancing in its springs of water,

It rounds in fish-shapes to flow,
In frogs to dance, and the dotted mucus
Everywhere in water like an eye of god,

Its black centre everywhere in limitless frog-pond.

ALL WET WITH DIAMONDS

When the Titanic breached its sides
With a roar of scrap iron and ice
And the collarless lascars drowned,
The Captain kept afloat
For five hours on the wings of his collar
The two Bishops for one hour longer
By the lifebelts around their neck,
The women survived by dancing in deep water
For the sake of their diamonds.
Those who had no diamonds, died
In a thunder of 9,000 soupspoons
Ringing in spindrift down the tinny corridors
With which RMS Titanic passed from the British Registry
    of Ships,
The Captain upheld by his uniform
The preachers by hot air in their cassocks
And the women paddling on silver dollars big as the Moon
In a jangle of 'change from the buoyant pound.

FROGS

The frogs croaking on the rockery, crying
'Brothers! Brothers!', with their fine thighs.

The frog at spawning-season clasped my thumb,
I had to wear him, like a green stone on a ring,
He would have waited everlastingly for eggs from my thumb,
I slid him loose in the water, his arms were strong.

They are something between a green chicken that hops
And a trap-jawed dog, and as their droplets grow
In the warm scummy ponds their proto-tadpoles
Are like our coiled beginnings in the womb
Arranged in necklaces and jelly-masses,

But black instead of white, like commas,

In multitudes, like sooty rain.

STONE TITLE

The stone-headed snail with its glass spoor.
The spiders run up their slack sails
On the Serpentine yacht's carved rigging. The mansion
Like an empty snail, stone candelabra
Too heavy to lift; stone coffers,
The lids too heavy to open; under the dust
Stone overcoats on the hall-stand,
Stone pens and stone writing-paper that cannot be folded,
A stone butler and a titled stone host lead me
To stone prayers with bread that is stones
Stone hymnbooks and stone wine and stony priest,
For someone has died and the stone body
Has died again into something heavier, so heavy

27

Its breath is stone that fills the stone house
And turns us to stone: the stone prayers
Are too heavy for jaws to lift, the stone music
Clatters in columns from the organ and we could be planted
In the stone graveyard as tombs of ourselves
Our stone passports open at our toes,
Above us the yews that have made a million leaves
Running on the wind ten thousand nights,
Whose roots grapple headstones and break
The tombs open like stone loaves.

THE SMITH'S ANVIL

A cow's placenta thrown over a whitethorn,
The daughter's placenta buried under the vine;
The cow slinks her calf, the ewe
Warps her lamb. Our stallion serves:

A white-washed wall ahead of his bolting eyes;

We want white in the coat. In the magical salon,
Or on the picnic, what feathers shall the father wear,
What masks, what pictures thrown on the bed's ceiling?

The rain is coming. Listen to the horses
Rattling their chains. The smith
Changes old iron into new. What he does

Sings with his blows for ever afterwards.

POET AND SMITHY

The shadows over the brickwork
In the warmth of the forge
Like writing almost appearing.
The men not held to account
For what they spoke at the forge
Among the red-hot ringing,
The ammonia of the quenching,
The white stains above the quenching-pots;
The patient animal treading on his white clouds
Like Pegasus; the poet not held to account.

FOSSILS
(*Cornish museum*)

A charge of canister-shot along the deck of the Frenchman.
Boatswain Bull received a shot which passed through both
    cheeks.

A West Indian, off Flushing, laden with
Rum, sugar, indigo and white cotton, foundering,

The beaches sticky for weeks, the tides
Rolled the cotton into blue sugar-balls, fluffy

Useless sweetmeats that clogged the buoys; look,
Here is one on the sill, dried hard as mahogany.

And the view, the cemetery, the stones worn by armies
Ebbing and slashing, jostling with their broadcloth the oldest
    stones

Streaked with sword-marks, and you could see the night-battle
Sparkling from across the river, like a tinder-box.

The younger stones chipped by musket-balls, the youngest
Awaiting their riveting charge of shrapnel. On show

Numerous portable mortalities: the skeleton
Head cleft in half with one of those sword-cuts,

A full money-belt about his empty loins;
The skeleton of a child crushed flat as a letter

Under the rusty cannon; here Nelson lay
Preserved in rum on his way to London; look at this slate,

A jelly-fish like a bullet-splash in the slab,
A million-year date-stamp; on this trestle rested

Wide-eyed in honey, golden Alexander.

IN THE CUTTING

Stiff moths of rust spread wing
Over the old cyclotron
Wedged in the railway cutting.
Ports welded, bolted,
A mile-long fuselage;
But I know what grows
Where matter parted and glittered
Where it sped so fast
Atoms turned into light:

The old spider is cramming
With gossamer the cyclotron
And his velleities muffle
The unused atomic chapel
And where sweating science
Prayed for scintilla,
Clematis tangles shadow,
Dust does its tango.

GOODS-TRAINS, BADS-TRAINS

Twenty-nine iron wagons full of clean stone.
The Railway is a beautiful metal
Staffed by sincere men
Who wear their uniforms handsomely.
The seamed face of the driver is a map
With the railways clearly marked.
His assistant has his grasp on the throttle.
The clean stone is going to be shaved
Into facings for nurseries, for swimming-baths,
Or some disinterested sculptor has ordered it
To enter, chiselling out his life's work.
There are no partings on this railway,
Only deliveries and meetings.
But when we are all met together
There must be another railway that takes us apart:
Lichened freight, that is already written with dates,
Insincere uniforms, with rucked seams, a driver
With longer experience whose face-bone shows no map,
The rail-irons a clanging skeleton over all England.

TO THE POSTMASTER GENERAL

He took the great bunch of letters and kissed it!
All those green stamps on the blue envelopes and on the
    white ones,
All those windowed debits and who knows a draft of credit,
All those missives sleeved in addresses and advertisements;
He grabbed the great bundle of envelopes off the mat and
    kissed it!
It proved the abundance of the world and his presence in it,
He blessed the postman and tossed them into the wardrobe,
Hung up his postman's uniform, and went out to fish,
Where silver creatures stamped with black and gold

Containing messages confined to issues of life and death
Swarmed, wrote and re-wrote themselves, fed, hatched and
    died
In the green-raftered halls of the water's sorting-office;
In the cool balsamic halls the watching flocks hung
Or turned swiftly to a new address: Blooded Worm, Esq.,
One A, Barbed Hook, The Line, Bankside: like letters with
    wings
Or a postman hurrying in his flowing pouch adventurous
    correspondence written
With energy and light on each leaf of the stacked flesh-pages.

HEADS AND TAILS

He on the head and she on the coin's tail:
Spin the coin upright on the table
They are running towards each other;
Flip the coin to decide a question: one or the other.
We spend the consorts in every shop,
They leave us they return to us
In several colours, in many sizes,
In every transaction. A person
Murders for their images; a person
Builds hospitals and pays doctors with them;
Where do they live, shall I ever meet them?
I earn them, or my father leaves them to me.

AUTOBIOSTEOGRAPHY

When he was dug up his bones were found covered
With fine minute cursive writing which when rubbed
With lampblack stood out like a crabbed inventory that was
Notes for an autobiography composed as though he stood

In his bones with his flesh over his arm with his limp head
Reading what he had written over the everlasting portion of
    him;
It seemed to have been scratched with the diamond-point
Found loose in the grave at the site of the heart.
I thought that all bones had their life-story graved on them
Like a stony map of how I have used my flesh;
He did conscientiously what no one can escape:
Leaving stone maps of judgment. However, he
After writing that composition passed into the museum
    gallery
Where millions of soft gazes like a stream wear his bones
    away.
Dickens signed soiled collars on his American tours. Hosts
Pass through the sea, utterly changed, unscathed, without
    writing a word.

SHAVING

I regard the wet brown eyes in the stubbled mask,
Why do we all wake to the day in turfy masks?

I wet the face, I pat it, I energise its roses,
I begin the day by scraping off the dead layer of the night.

My face floats expanded in a concave dish of mirror,
Perfumed, embalmed, stung to life again,
A little streak of red mingling with the cologne.

Men with beards are wild men!
They stand around in their tangles of slumber and growth!

The shaven man learns anew who he is each sunrise
By standing in his own full view watching his own expression

For ten minutes while the blade sweeps away the blue-black
  embers
Of the night's fires; the tempered blade, Samurai! the face is
  born.

These faces rise into the mirror blue-black as from death's
    bruises;
Lazarus had a deep stubble of eleventh-hour shadow:

But he emerged from the cave super-fatted, shining with
    glory,
And beardless as a baby, his Jesus tomb-barbered him.

GORGON GRAVE
(*White Monument*)

This heroine, sword-handed, marble-lipped,
Rigid curls tumbled out of a tall helmet,
In the low hiss of church heating, eyes
Heavenward; I think with gaze averted they caught the Gorgon
And bolted over her angry snakes that stretched appalled
A silver inside-polished casque; this warrior
Stretches her mouth for a brave shout
As the whiteness spreads, the contagious stone.
Church has her caught in marble, under the stone hat
Snakes locked bolt-eyed in the hollow mirror.

AFTER THE CRASH

My soapy meditation in my still-colliding bathtub.
I am all blurred, I am warm soapy water;
Hard edges are for dead people,
Like the breadloaf that cannot be holographed

Because it is moving, gently heaving,
Living even when sliced, cannot stay still
Till it is staled and corpsed; and the face
That hangs like a blurred mask
Behind the ruby hum, the laser,
That is an alive face: it is a trembling curtain.

The roads full of cars, pouring metal
With beating oily streams of air above
Like the syllable Graaaa endlessly pronounced,
Blurred from living death, the metal slightly blurred
With vibration, beating with hot air, then
As the solid car touches the solid car, the final
Dead stop with all the sound of the world in it,

A bird-call and a volcano, a soprano and a hammer,
All the possible tunes of metal, the trombone in the foundry,
And the mark of the sound wadded into a flat conch impact.

I lost nothing but an old tooth.
I rode the ambulance with the new moon like a keel
In hard-edge of the deadboat of souls above me.
I wash the oily skin and sound of the metal off,
I buzz still in my skin like those grinding hulls,
I see the water roughen in the buzzing bath,
Soap-clouds spread, the steel mantra dies.

The metal bees have sought their garages.
We are their honey and pollen, the sweet thing
They gather and destroy, the flesh-roses.

THE BOMBS

He pissed himself, his tears ran down his legs,
He was unable to cross the road for weeping people.

35

The bomb exploded in the Supermarket.
No one was hurt. All the food

Was blown out of the cans in a glistening mess,
All the tins quite empty on their shelves, trembling.

The other bomb went off during choir practice
In the church and everybody was hurt.

Many will not sing again after that shout.
I could not cross the road for weeping people.

One woman saying over and over:
Jesus has been here to lead the Innocents home,

Jesus has been here to lead the Innocents home.
There were bloody footsteps in the chancel,

Blood and brains in the lap of the Virgin,
The small cakes of Jesus were ground into the firemen's
    water.

The stone of the tombs was stained but quite dry,
As though the tombs had drunk thirstily.

Gristle in the pulpit, a large piece
Stuck on the wooden desk where the Bible had been.

The face blown off one boy, his raw skull
Smiled quiet above the crisp white ruffles of surplice.

None of the stained glass had been broken
Though the great doors were off in the West;

The unruffled Saints glowed around the glass crucifixion.
Jesus stepped out of his tomb just beneath the surface.

I wanted Innocents trooping into the glass picture,
Identical naked children stripped of their flesh

Stripped of their bones, for the choir stalls
Were packed full with the lips and the bones,

The headlong choirmaster buried in his machine.
They scrubbed the church but it should not have been
    touched,

It should have been left corrupting
With the good flies and their worms busy as a congregation

Of the people in a flash turned into torn bread for them
As a picture-sight for the times,

Photographed, and sold on railway stations
At all the resorts to flavour the holiday seaside,

Says Seamus, to flavour the icecreams and the innocent
    lemonade;
A perfume bottled and sold called Reek of the Innocents,

One dab behind the ear creates a deathshead.

PRINTS OF THE DEAD

The Printer in the town: as his wife entered
Her final illness, the paper he chose
For each piece of work got heavier,
More opulent. He spoke of his
'Better half', meaning his dog.

The tombs were full of soundless tunnels,
Full of pips sprouting through the bowels,
Full of eyes that split and lungs adrift in pus,
Full of tree-roots tunnelling in through the meat;

The dead do not look at such things, they have more
        important matters,
They have been taken up into some magnificence,
As oil spreads rainbow tents across water,
The dead are like rainbows that filth makes;

Only the practised dead
Those who have done it again and again
Bother to remember, and drift sometimes
In a bristling perfume, a skirted scent-tone
They once wore, from a shaded canopy they have been
        building;
Or in wasp-clothes foray from some apple they've been
        dismantling,
Or in bee-dress arranging weddings of pollen, falter,
Remember.

I smell the beards of the dead in this ancient panel,
I should recognise them I had a beard like this myself,
I was there once, among friends and fellow-workers;

Look! that grain is a long-section of a wooden beard,
There is a footprint forming slowly in the grain,
Look, that knot has my fingerprints, the same loops,
The same whorls. Inspector! arrest that dead man,
He is hiding in the secret room's panelling.

RED INDIAN CORPSE

Deer-of-the-Waters: he laboured hard on his grammar
And learnt to say John Doe; his coat of arms of a deer
Went back to the Stone Age: the family mark,
The dodaim or totem which was his true father
And everyone's true father, since the pregnant women
Fed on venison, and this built his body; the red flesh
Of all his ancestors was this same totem venison.

Then they did the Italian Pope Trick on him:
Confessed him, shot him, and as one might say
John O'Woman, called him after the totem: Doe,
Typed on a tag-label tied to his left big toe.

GEORGE NEVER RESTS

The green wireless in the churchyard, laying down
Its recordings, its stacked reels, the stepped
Stairs of the green bluffs, the continual wind.
Inside the church, gloom, but quiet, the old wood
Of the pews laid to rest, and behind
The inscribed stone slabs total quiet:
Silently breaking silence a turmoil window,
The only window: St George in silver
Fighting a green-and-gold dragon that lapped him
That must have broiled him with its breath
Playing on his metal suit, and it held him still,
But then the wind started up again
And the shadows in that window struggled
And St George roasted in a hearth of black flames
Where he writhed with a dragon and stabbed
Again and again at the undying worm, and he throws
Down his sword and great stripes scar his face
And he has his sword again in the deaf windows of the
    church.
The wind rolls out to sea in its coils,
It circles the globe, it has never heard of St George.

GOD SAYS 'DEATH'

God says 'Death' in a gentle voice
To the corpse sleepless with the wheats

That hiss on a low earth-note all night
Like a door hung over with dark leaves
Out of which the immense syllable blows:
'Death' in God's voice dressed in his spiderweb shirt
With its tassels of wheat, in his knobbly dressing-gown
Pulled from the oak; he
Says 'Death' with all his clothes,

And his mushroom buttons,
And his ponds which are mirrors
Tunnelling into the sky where he jumps up
Parting the thundercloud with electrical claws;

The reedy marshes of the railway, on some platform
Deep in East Anglia with the mire-drummer thumping
Through the lonely sky, God might pop out of the mud
Puffing a smoke rolled of flesh, dung and pelt,
And offer me one

And I could ask him then why 'Death',
And he would smile like a dago in his black cloak,
And offer me life to keep quiet about it,
'Would you call God a liar?' he hands me flowers
From the churchyard: 'Do you call these dead?'

CERBERUS

Cerberus terra est et consumptrix
Omnium corporum; the soup that gives
A nasty bite; the daffodils
That have sunlit teeth; sugar-skulls
Left sticky on the nursery bookshelf;
The grains of dust which are fulfilments.

The friend and eater of corpses,
The dog which salivates over its bowl:

I leave myself to this dog, I
Will continue to nourish him.
The wheels turn and the lanterns light themselves,
This ramshackle graveyard and old folks' home,
This ramshackle quiet graveyard where the dead are feasting,

The great grass-bearded head presides.

You take turns to be food,
Before you can grind wheat you have to be wheat,
Before you can eat bread you are a nice new crust
Eaten by Mary, who chooses a crust-you here,
A mouthful of Shakespeare's breath there, a glass
Of transparent Genghis Khan there, with her teeth
She strips a seed that multitudes have built:

The kindness striving through her whole body
Yet she eats the dead, as you do,
Dead-body pasties, the skull full of pus-custard,
The fast-shut face baked brown as a loaf by the dry sand;
The long pig stuffed with choiring energies

Sings for nine months her Jesus into her;

We wear worm-masks that cover our real faces
As the worms do; I leave myself to a cats' home,
The last testament of Peter Catsmeat;

He changes his name to John Bonio

Preferring in his beliefs the workmanlike fraternity of dogs,
Not as I do the more private sorority of cats.

'ER
(*For P.B.*)

They call the Bulls "Er!' 'I's a-going to see 'er fuck,'
"Er's got a chill from the wet pasture,' "Er's worth
All the farm put together,' and this a tobacco-brown bull
With tight rust-curls between neat moon-horns,
A dewlap like the Chancellor's wig, and a pizzle
Like Adam-tongue for 'thrust': in 'Er's herd
Among 'Er's wives and so much chewing inwardness,
'Er's pizzle orders the meadows, as thunder does.
Bo-opis potnia Here: 'cow-eyed Mistress Hera . . .'
'Era can't be a Bull! So I watch 'Er's eyes:
They are the eyes of a cow, but bright with purpose:
Now 'Er sees 'Era's purpose among 'Er's cows,
And all eyes brighten, the cows like rogues scamper,
The Farmer rubs his hands, the cow-rider mounts
Like shunting trains, and like meadow-thunder
Hero serves Hera in the trampled grass that seeds.

VICARAGE MOONCAKES

The white pillar of water throws itself
Over the inlet cliff. What keeps the Moon up?
Nothing but itself, rolling over the ground,
Luminous millstone. The Vicar has made a clock
Out of balsa-wood and black soapstone,
He has a pair of pants of black bible-leather,
He has a parson's leather-jacket marked Holy
Across the shoulders, and Bible on the bum;
He has made a walking-stick
Of plaited straw: he likes featherlight things.
He lies on Fridays in a special bed
Which is a wooden plank in his large dry hall.
He writes a long letter to his Bishop, cold as a prison corridor.

He feeds a death's-head moth on a piece of marzipan:
He is an authority. The Moon
Grinds soft white flour over his parsonage,
The daily round bakes him like a loaf of crust,
And he feeds us with Jesus like little soft moonstones
That taste of marzipan from his lepidopterist's fingers.

THE GRAND LUNACY

The moon is the mansion of the mighty mother,
With its one blazing window it wings across the sky,
It is the abyss, sensing everything,
It is the opener, pulling up the frail spirit,
Snapping its rootlets a little more, each time.

Its glassy beverage, sticky as libido,
Oozes out of the mistletoe,
My moon-yolk leaps out into the bedroom,
Moon-beam, self-coloured.

The dead are the embryo people of the earth,
They are called Demetrians, eternal freshness
Is guaranteed for them; as the moon passes
They all stand on tiptoe, her beams
Comb them, they are like cobwebby wheat
As the wheat is, with its indefinite stalks,
Its frayed alleys of shadows, bending, tiptoe.

It is she who causes the woman's tongue in my mouth
To branch like an antler, and the wings of cupid
Deep in my body, to beat; it is she
Who twines her fingers in my skin,
Flays a layer as one pulls
A sheet off a mirror in which she stares

From the one window flying in the sky of her stone cottage.

43

PARSON'S ROCK

Sheer terror of rock-rose pounds down the cliffs.
The moth that feeds on the rose bears raw head
And bloody bones on its wings. Even now he is dead
His gaze is turned down only a little.
I saw him when he preached, and his gaze was turned up
So far I can still see him plainly with my eyes closed.
The mountain wears a grey shawl over grey cliffs.
Wispy clouds hang and shape its shoulders in the early light.
By the waterfall, I wish I could sketch. Since his death
I see him everywhere, in clouds, in water, he has splashed
To millions of him when he collided with death
Whose gaze was turned up. Every parson
With barred throat and black chest wears his uniform.
Every open mouth in a distant crowd
Sings psalms like him within me,

And though the waterfall is nothing like,
Nor the mountain anything like him,
The smallest boulder wet with mountain fall
Grows to a parish church, grey as the rocks where mountain
    climbers
Rope themselves on towers and pinnacles
Seeking entrance to the mountain with their gazes
Turned up looking for footholds, their mouths wide
As though singing psalms that love the rock
And comprehend it with pitons, throwing across
A shirt of climbing-ropes so that it is a god
Like his cloud-shawled *Ein feste Burg* where
Rock-rose gathered on the cliff-brink turned up death's gaze.

SEAN'S DESCRIPTION

The grave of the careless lady who swallowed pips,
From the rich subsoil of her stomach and snapped coffin-
    timbers
A fine greasy crop of apples glittering

With their waxes; and Sean told me
Over a customary glass the best description he'd read
Of what a dead person looked like, actually:

'A green doughnut with eyeholes in it,' he said,
'A green doughnut with black cream,' as we sat

By the waterlilies rooted in mud of the pub garden,
And a bumble-bee in a tippet of glossy fur
Snatched a line from the air, and I brought
One of her apples from my pocket, and bit
Through the sweet flesh that fizzed with young ciders
And my toothmarks blazed white through the red skin.

'Look,' I said, holding up another firm sweet apple,
'This is what a dead person really looks like; taste her.'

THE LOOMS OF THE ANCESTORS

Cloth woven on a loom whose spindle-weights
Are made of the sliced bones
Of forefathers and foremothers.
The loom is the burial place of the ancestors:
The long bones for the treadles,
The sliced bones for the weights,
The thin bones carved into the shuttles.
As each person dies, some portions
Are fed to the birds,

The remainder buried in the cotton-fields,
The bones boiled and varnished,
Carved, and pegged with bone-nails
Into the loom, which is called
By the person's real name, which is not used
When they are alive, but is their loom-name.
Some flesh flies in the air, other meat
Is buried wrapping cotton-seeds,
This harvest also bears their name and is woven
On the loom of their bones which is placed
In the courtyard where the birds drink.
The garment is called by the relationship.
I am wearing my grandfather's aunt on my back.
My first wife is these knickers.
Sheep graze on the cemetery grass
Where the wool-people are buried, not far from the hills
Where we white cotton-people burst our pods.
When the sheep are filled, the goats graze there,
We ferment their milk to a spirit
Which speaks through the shaman's lips
Drunk on ancestors. The chief wears
A robe of woollen chiefs, many-layered as an umpire,
And the birds feed from his grandmother mittens.

I spin my father's white flesh onto my wife's fast wheel.

BELIEFS

The dead appear to us as they were at their prime.
As men die snakes undulate through the floor.
One of them copulates with the body: the child
Of this union is the soul, or apparition.

I wear a headdress with a tassel
Containing two enemy skulls known as
The testicles: they are heavy. Our prize yams

46

Are adorned with long-nosed masks. My Queen's vulva
Is thoroughly tattooed with our scriptural index:
She is the Concordance. From infancy
Her labia have been stretched by systematic
Sucking and pulling: we give this job
To the impotent old men:
It cheers their retirement.
I was once left for dead in the bush after a battle,
And my testicles stolen, that is to say
My crowning scrotum, but I revived
When I felt a woman urinating on me, accidentally:
It was my Queen. We make furious love
Inside the Concordance, and, sleeping with her, I am sure
To rise on the day of battle with my erection firm,
My virile member with its distinctive bent end,
And she protects the mud-track to my house
By naming it after her long outer lips.
We have mudhead drums that seem to contain
A butterfly you can hear in the music
Which imparts erotic madness: we have elephants
Fat as monsoon clouds; we have
A tree ritually killed and brought back to life,
The sun and the moon in its branches; and my ancestor
Killed tigers in the forest without interrupting
Intercourse: he drew a deep bow. One day
They will leave me to the snakes and my soul
In its manly prime but with the knowledge-organs
Of man and woman will enter the cave
Of Agua Bendita, and I shall stand beneath

The blessed semen from the stalactitic penes,
And I shall grow very slowly in my soul-size
Sheathed with thin stone, mite to stalagmite,

Will join the council of the elder stones
Crowned everlastingly with the ointment of the rocks

Shining with the water that conceived the rocks.

OPEN-HEADED

The Deity appears
As a tree that will not keep still in the wind

As a tree that has always been there since babyhood,
I touch this tree and I touch the Deity

That bark rough as ancient walls to my touch;
We are the babies of the plant kingdom.

I speak to my mother, she is pleased that I remember her.
Her house rustles through its 365 rooms, I leave her.

Alive, the weather moves me hard. Dead,
It will slide me apart like chess-pieces.

On the beach I watch the jelly salt squads
Of fringed wheels that star-stud the tide

With sexual opulence, beating, beating; my nosebleed
Stopped when I leant my back's length against the
    crocodilian bark,
It has dried like beetles' wing-cases.

PLACE

The train's brakes lowing like a herd of cattle at sunset
As it draws up by Lesson's Stone, by mountains
Like deeply carved curtains, among small birds
Knapping at the stationmaster's crumbs, hopping-black
Like commas of wet ink: I could see their small eyes glisten.
I thought I must die in my sleep, I lay in my bunk
Like wet clothes soaking, the convulsions were the journey,

48

The bedroom bumped. I stepped off and the mountain
    landscape
Was like stone guests set round a still table
On which was set stone food, steaming
With the clouds caught on it; a plateau
Surrounded with peaks and set with cairns
And stone houses, and a causeway up to Giant's Table,
And the railway trailing like a bootlace. My house
Was hard by Lesson's Stone, near the sparkling Force
That tumbled off the cliff, that in summer
Left its dry spoor full of thornbush. Then the lizards
Flickered among the rocks, like shadows
Of flying things under a clear sky, or like
Bright enamelled painted rock on rock, until they swiftly
Shot sideways too fast to see. I arrived
On Lesson's Stone Stop platform a decade ago;
The place where I live is still like pieces
Of a shattered star, some parts shining
Too bright to look at, others dead
As old clinker. I am afraid to mention
The star's name. That would set it alight.

VILLAGE TALK

In the street the dead are visiting,
They do not look at me, their faces are deeply folded
And their eyes drilled with deep black holes
Whose axis they follow like ramrods.
How does that gaze alight? I would not meet it.
One of them raps the front door opposite.
Mrs Change greets the tall silent visitor kindly,
Ushers him into the fire-lighted parlour
With the large flowers blazing on the wallpaper,
And through the window I see them chatting, animated
Before she crosses and draws the curtain.
A rap sounds at my own front door, I must answer

A deeply-folded grey face, a tall figure;
I beckon it inside, I smile, I show it to the fireside,
It needs to warm itself, I enquire about the journey,
Now it starts talking to me rapidly and with pleasure
Twice as fast as a live person visiting,
He has more to tell, more stored up,
The visits of the dead are bountiful.
I pour my visitor a small glass of apple-brandy,
He lifts it and drinks with a powerful smile,
His face has bronzed and I turn a bar of the fire off
He claps me on the shoulder we are good pals
He undoes his case I see it is packed with quartz crystals
He presses this flashing souvenir on me
He takes his leave I am left breathless
He walks past the window grey face folded
Eyes drilling to their destination, lucky fellow.

WASP-FOREST

I

Forestry, you call a weed by name, and check it.
You murder the beetle that devours the wasp.
The wasp-plague begins, the horses are stung,
Plunging, the squire's daughter is thrown.
The wasps have dragged her underground
And dressed her in their papery clothes.

II

They make their nests of your papered clothing
I saw one crawling on your wedding-gown
In his jaws a white crumb of your wedding-weeds.
I found one in the filing-drawer,
They eat paper, it had been at the red birth-certificates.
Let them have an allowance. We did, until this plague.

My library is being cannibalised by their papery cities,
Their pot-bellied cities full of fanning wings,
The cities where they grow their poisons
And sound their *Oms* under the shady
Ink and paper of my Swift and Shakespeare.

III

They'll have a book down to its juiceless core
All white and cavernous like dug-out apples;
They do not get drunk on books, they stagger out of apples
Like rose-pillared pubs at closing-time, soar
Up out of the alcoholic bruises: Applebees,
Applecrabs, Applesharks, my striped Captain,
My gold-black Flower, my Loverwasp.

IV

Atoms are little notes sung as by wasps in wasp city.
Wasps live in paper as a book does.
Books in a manner are nests of wasps
Living together and hung with stings. Smoke out this library,
Leave the books all blank as albums: see!
The words are coughing, coughing themselves
On their backs all over the college table.
Do not touch this half-dead cougher
His other half of life is in his sting.
Like a short fuse, it contains anti-matter,
Anti-flesh, a little quill which is a seashore of fever.

V

There is the wasp-nest, we have tracked it down,
Half clung to the brick and half to the panelling
We tracked its hum through the wooden corridors
Our ears to glass tumblers. We have killed them
Honest Cyanide hath ta'en order for't
The big nest hangs like a paper vase

Like a papier-mâché mask of a prophetic head
We tear it from the masonry and shake corpses out of it.

Which of us would stand without cyanide, listening
For oracle to arise out of *Om* of Paper City
Made of books and wedding-dresses and birth-certificates?
Who would be wasp-sacrificed to the grey head's
Courts, galleries, alleys black with wings;
Shall we tweezer them back into their layers and tombings?
It will not speak again, and we have silenced this oracle
    following:

Singing paperhouse in woodenhouse among talking trees.

TRIPPED

A charged-wire cattle-fence by the church
As though the rain strung like an abacus
Were glass bees settled on it, buzzes; I touch it

I am on my back. I have been thrown
I have been tripped without believing it
By an electrical judo-master
Who has thumped me with the soft ground
Who has dirtied my shoulders. I kick in air
Like a fly in orgasm, the cold brown water
Interesting my spine, the glass bees buzzing.

I think of the cattle, with their conductive noses,
Their salt tongues: it will strike them down
The fields littered with wet pink foetuses
Like pigmy cattle that are fish
Struggling to breathe.

The farmer's wife, his babies,
The trespassing lover,

All lie on their backs by the lines of glass bees,
Foaming like epileptics — and the epileptics who touch it!

I will cross this field from the North. Some inventor,
That nun enriched by the barbed-wire of Flanders,
Is still drawing dividends, I see from the stretch
Of vile stars in silent strings of rust.

At the farmhouse we feast
On dumplings, dripping-bread,
Cushiony crumpets satined with butter,
Suet sweet with syrup, fatty ham,
And hot toast damasked with wall-plums;

Whose starchy wife takes a stiff brush
To my soiled shoulders, my buzzing back; chirping boxes

Are sunny CHICKS BY CARRIAGE in the yard.

LIGHTNING LEAP

Eyes as flowers, tears as stems.
The rocks, grinding, rebound,
They spark in the avalanche,
Lightening along the scree,
Lightening under the snow

That rolls like a sea-foam
Like the foam on a tsunami
With lightning leaping in it
In mile-long bolts
Over the landgrave and the landgravine,
Over the husking and winnowing places,
Over the bell still hot from its warning,
Over the ringers with their brass breaths,
Over the woman proud of her sweetness,

The Murderess, white as snow,
Over the butchers'-girls in white aprons
With their silver knives skinning the white fat,
Over the house with the black well and the oak,
Over the thousand sheep and the old pale whiskey,
Over the ski-slopes and the whitegallon dairies,

As though lightning had cut down the great snow tree
And with its uncountable leaves it came swishing.

GUARDED BY BEES

The pornographic archives guarded by bees
Who have built comb in the safe; iron doors
From which the honey drips; I sip a glass
Of bee-sherry, yellow and vibrant; I came here
Past the old post-office, boarded up,
From within the cool darkness sun-razored
I heard the hum of bees; my friend tells me

That the radioactive cities of the future
Will be left standing for euthanasia,
They will be kept beautiful though all trees
And lawns will be plastic. Those who wish to die
Will drift through the almost-empty streets,
Loiter through the windows of the stores,
All open, all untended, what they fancy they can take,
Or wander through the boulders of Central Park, its glades
To hear the recorded pace and growl in the empty zoo-cages,
And consider the unperturbed fountains of water,
While it, and they, are rinsed through and through
As the pluming spray by sunlight, with killing rays,
Lethal broadcasts, until they can consider no more.
Germs over the whole skin die first, the skin after,
Purity first, then death, in the germless city that amazes
The killed lovers with its pulsing night-auroras.

I reply I would prefer a city constructed of OM,
A city of bees, I want this disused city
Converted to a hive, all the skyscrapers
Packed with honeycomb, and from the windows
Honey seeping into the city abysses, all the streets
Rivers of cloudy honey slipping in tides,
And the breeze of the wings as they cool our city.

This would be my euthanasia, to be stung by sweetness,
To wander through the droning canyons scatheless at first,
Wax thresholds stalagmited with honey-crystals
I snap off and munch, and count the banks
That must brim with the royal jelly . . .

And some wander through the sweet death, city of hexagons
And are not stung, break their hanging meals off cornices
In the summer-coloured city, drink at the public fountains
Blackened with wings drinking, and full of wonder
Emerge from the nether gates that are humming
Having seen nature building;
                                          others stagger
Through the misshapen streets, screaming of human glory,
Attended by black plumes of sting,
With a velvet skin of wings screaming they're flayed.

SOME ANIMALS

I

'God encompasseth us . . .' 'What did you say?'
'I said "See you at the Goat-and-Compasses." '
The dog limps into the Church.
It is uncertain: is this an inside
Or is it an outside? There is so much emotion here
Reeking in the pillars. It is not a dwelling-place,
Yet people spend much time here, howling and feeding.

There are trees of stone standing, and trees on their sides
To sit in, in which the people suddenly at a sound
Fall on all-fours. They make a choking scent
Like a bonfire, by burning herbs, and a light in the air
From candles, and as the little bell rings
There is a faint edge-on scent which is unforgettable.
Is it the smell of Christ, can a dog see Him
In the nose? The dog kneels,
The priest flings him a Host, it flies
Like a full moon and dog snaps it out of the air.

II

The toad sprouts feathers, every wart a gem.
It gazes out of its plumage impassively
Like an Indian chief with a feather shawl.
The Batrachians are honoured this week, rightly so:
Ten big black-and-white frogs like humbugs on a bedspread.
Spiders have turned vegetarian, a great one
Roams above our town, bends like a harbour crane for its
    long grass,
Munches it like a stork, cruises at two storeys
Creaking, perfumed like a hayloft.
The ravens, though, have got dandruff;
It is the bad food, and the lack of meaty spiders.
My wife passes mice through the squeaky mincer,
Puts out the nice mice-mince for the ravens' dandruff.
I take my dog to the Goat-and-Compasses
For a raven-backed Guinness.

III

Great flocks of butterflies like wheeling, flexing rainbows,
Like fluttering heat-haze that can see and lay eggs,
Spanning oceans on a few drops of sugar-water,
And the dense suet of their bygone caterpillar.

IV

The lava larvae that tunnel the pumice
To warm their gems at the roots of geysers,
Imagos that dodge the eruption-boulders,
Or couple on still-glowing platforms of hurtling rock;
Their maggots wriggle all over the lava-flows;
Their steel beetle-wings clash in subterranean gales.

V

The moles like furry bulldozers crumbling rock.
They canter like racehorses when I stamp,
Down turdy corridors; they do not trouble
With thin surfaces, they are birds of the deep earth.
They drink belly-up the sweet rain that falls through roofs
Of branches, roofs of flowers, roofs of grass, root-roofs,
Until they are so full of sweetness they rot and breed
     butterflies.

VI

All the animals vote to make up a great and wonderful maiden
With eyes and jaws at every joint
Who can read, and bite like a pack of animals,
Who can take tea, and pose for bathing-pictures,
Who can break up into howling runners
At the slightest threat and surround it;

Who can dream as the pack dreams, singleton;
Who can fuck as the pack fucks, multiplex.

EN ROUTE IN TOPPERS TO ASCOT

He is going to horse-worship at the Races.
Everything about him refers to horses,

He carries glasses in horse-leather cases,
His chest is buttoned into a horse-leather waistcoat,

His shoes are shining brightly
As horse-sweat after a race,

He is the worshipper of the Horse
Dressed in the bodies of winners;

Once a year they pull their spirits and their smiles,
Their whiskies and their pink gins,
Out of spirit bottles made of the leather of sires,
Feed at horse-steak restaurants
On distinguished runners, to become all horse.

His wife is dressed as flowers,
She wears a sun-hat which is a weather-spell,
Her face resembles her mother's —
Whom I have not met, but she
Would have to be her own ancestor to look so haughty —

His hat is grey as the horses of Venus,
As the eyes of Athena
Who rode a horse-chariot into the swamps of Hydra
Muddy as Epsom was, in its first spring rains.

Waterloo rises among its own mists:
The electric trains should on this day of days
Switch off and be drawn by teams of horses.

JABEZ DOG AGAIN

Jabez Dog meets a bitch
With lights along her tits, a bitch with the capability
That can differentiate between acetaldehyde and
Benzopyrene at a concentration of one in

One to the ninth power; but then
Meditates Jabez, all dogs are like that, even him.
Though instead of lights along his tits
He has them at cock and arsehole, with a great one
Within his nose, and his head resides between
Two hearing-searchlights that can distinguish
His master's snore from every rattle and squeak
Of the night-train just pulling out of Dundee
While Jabez has his leg cocked at Hampton Court
At the root of the Great Vine contributing
To its centuries-savour of the seldom English grape;
And in this skull also reside next to these crackling detectors
Soft brown and serviceable his poor dim eyes.

THRUST AND GLORY

A great longhaired hog, glistening with the dew,
It knows night by heart, sucked through blue irises,
But day it allows to rest and glitter on its skin
And its long hairs harsh as fingernails
Like coarse reeds on a hump of the bog.
It is a golden pig and its underslung rod
Is the very word for *thrust*, like the drill
Into the future, and it will run along that drill's sights;
But now, glistening with distillate, it waits
For the sun to raise moulds of steam along its back,
For the sun to warm it dry and the air to towel it
Testing its hooves meanwhile that clock on the stone,
Ready with its seed and tusks and bolts of muscle
And the grease of seed it pumps into the black sow
Like lightning-bolts into the hulking black thunder anvil
And the storm will gather until it breaks and rains pigs,
The mud glorious with rain-shine, pig-grease and wallow.

SWINISHNESS

I have dug up a pig's skull and there was a brass heart in the
 grave
The little clasp was fused but I chiselled the heart open
Inside was a letter its creases seamed with earthy water
Its writing nearly steamed away and cooked with
 decomposition
It said: there are many priests less human than this pig,
Return this memorial to earth with a thought for pigs.
And I thought of them thundering with madness over the
 cliffs
Pigs given thought and speech by that Jesus and so amazed
They fled into a bloody surf beating at the base of their
 pasture;
I thought of the pig that is life in death and vice versa
The ghost in the cottage of all the refuse that they throw out
Which sinks in the wallow and then walks in again on the
 pig's bones,
Including dung, its own dung and mine, and how out of that
And all other disjecta it makes its babies which we are glad to
 eat
Except for a selection of the litter which we keep for
 breeding.
There is when the milking mother has not enough tits to go
 round
And eats the poor starveling left over until the next time
And how she crunches the bones of her ancestors if she needs
 calcium
And how her boar's penis is the very syllable *thrust* underslung
Like a compact punctuation or rocket-missile in his square
 flank

Which seed is risen from the earth and grunts and squeals
 appallingly
In his worshipful fit of her which lasts a few seconds, I swear
 she grins;

And I take apple sauce with her younger daughter, and that
    gummer
Enters me and causes a mild ecstasy because she is truly
    delicious
And my underworld reduces her to Persephone who will
haunt the mud

Until her mother meets her in her mouth again and makes use
    of what I could not
And may appear on my plate next year in a castrated form as
    a rasher;
And I think of the Eleusinian initiates in their fine robes
Racing after greased pigs that escape into the sea
And how the foam is full, packed full, of squealing hymns.
Isis rode into the sea on a pig, its hooves galloping;
We cut its throat and plash its blood on the young marrieds
Or so it came to me in a dream once. In the butcher's
    window
The pig's head sits on its neck with its heavy eyes dreaming
Of splashing me with her blood as a token of good faith,
A sealed compact, and an earnest that when the Goddess
    appears to me
Wearing just such a pig's head, then that is her choice of
    energy,
And a matter of theology, and a covenant of resurrection in
    the flesh;
And she looks at me with Eve's eyes in the pig's head to test
    me
And since I am not afraid, not this time round,
And have left flinching, drops her, and my, disguise.

KEEPERS

The silvery water-peel speckled with blue,
The water-armour of the fish,
The feathering throats, a strong

61

Back-glow and shudder of purple as the fish turns,
Water-bloom on a sea-fruit, light-feathered water-birds,

The small faces hanging in the shop-window,
With snails like travelling padlocks scouring the glass.

Their proprietor sharpens a carving-knife on his threshold.
He carves live fish-masks from living trees.
He says he will one day go to visit the whale's graveyard,
Like white-washed churches littered over some unknown
    island:
Not for the sea-ivory but for the magnificence!
And the levee of whales mourning like a harvest of geysers.

The small motor strops above his tanks
As he sharpens his sculptor's mask-knives,
Gazing at the small faces feathered in their colours:

Tigerishly striped and dog-eyed,
Or eyes like wells of blackness
With crumpled foil of gold,
Or toad-eyed and smooth-skinned as rainbows,
Hanging like masks in their transparent halls:

Who looks back at him through these faces, the salt sea?

Away over in the waterworks, the Tap-Assistant
Converses every dawn with his great shackled charge.

BOX BOX

I *Music box*

He makes chests of tools of elm, polished pale wood,
Finely jointed like dolls' fingers holding each corner fast;

So perfect is his craftsmanship that if you squeeze
Such a box in your hand it gives off snatches of swift solemn
   music.

II *Tooth-box*

The Bach cantata that brought him suddenly to age
And realisation, no. 21; his milk-teeth pattered out
Like ripped shirt-buttons as he cried out 'Oh! I see . . .'
Are semi-lunar upper and lower rows fastened in elm gums
Of a box-model of his mouth secured with a hush-clasp.

III *Stink-box*

A scent-organ arranged in an elm-chest like a locked console
With a slippery polished bench to confront it; he chooses
To sniff Incense of Arson first, then the tremendous
Scent of Mahomet at Ramadan, and then a snuff made of
Colm shale, the odour of millions of years resting
In strata, and of fine-ground Devonian sandstone,
The vermilion earth-cellars of Exeter: he resolved to buy
A supply of geological snuff to evoke the place
Where he was made and the soil he first woke up in,
The white earth of a baby; he will pinch snuff before ever
Speaking, with his nose will touch his roots, like any dog,
Like Hardy's Father, dying, called for a glass
Of well-water to taste where he was.

IV *Ghost-box*

A chest of cheese-cloths for constructing ghosts, manufactured
From swathings of finest blue cheese that have grave-odour,
   grave-colour
Of delicate shine as it wafts on the medium's jointed rods;
Cheese is a sacred food since it shines and is edible decay;
The medium's tricks are holy pageant to those who eat cheese
Puzza come la natura d'una donna.

V *House-box*

He drinks the iridescent, deep-black, beetle-coloured wine
At midnight in the soughing halls of poplar
Through which the death's head courts its plain-fleeced mate;
His house behind him in the gloom is box-fitted,
The panelling is elm, and so are the pianos, his studs
Pistols and suits are shut in neat boxes, and tomorrow,
He will for a kissing-cousin walk her elm coffin with alack.
It is a good thing for trees his avenue cannot be jointed, is
    poplar.

SMITH AND MOTOR-CAR

The plunging iron flowers in ammonia-clouds.

His leather apron and his gauntlet hands,
His heaps of coal that glow like piled riches,
His horny singing anvil, his top-heavy hammer
Of clean iron falling with a clean note,
The horse standing on a cloud
Of hoof-smelling steam.

               My motor-car
Skinned with headlit images on the road
Of clotted metal from Penzance to Chiswick;
The dragon-breath that kills the judging oak,
The one snake of a million scales, each scale
With doors and mirrors and a set of quartz-beams.

At Marazion, a man with a bag of tools in his hand
Strolling up a lane towards the moon.

I shall melt my car down into a splendid microscope,

The smith shall hammer and bend it to a plough.

THE WHOLE MUSIC AT POD'S KITCHEN

While eating a crisp ice-cold lettuce at Pod's Kitchen
I thought of how the white flesh of cumulo-cirrus was ice,
How wind pulled the fronds from the seven-mile lettuce
That hovered daintily over counties, wide as a county,

I thought of how the thunderstorm whirls the white
    blanketings,
How the sheer-white terraces become a palace of fireworks
Like a Snowdon aviary of rainbows spreading their wings
And sparking their beaks and fucking in great thumps;

I find on my green lettuce
A tiny snail like hard snot

I think of poisons so old
That they have become precious stones
Pulling back to black earth edible men and women
And how the earth folds over them like grave thunderbulks
With white inscriptions startling in the dusk.

I swallow my edible green fronds and regard
My glass of water fallen from those clouds
In black thunder;

It stands still and clear, poised to enter me,
Like one long distinct note of the whole music.

CARE OF FLORA

This tree's fruit
Is of a most disgusting stench and the most delicious flavour.
All must uncover in the presence of the clove-trees.
When the rice is in bloom, we fire no guns.

65

This tree looks after the village.
Regard its branches, they are a model of the forking streets.
If you want to know where to get to and where you have
    come from
The tree is the globular map; stand here and understand.

We built the haunted houses with haunted trees.
If we want to cut the grove, we build a small house first,
Furnish it with little clothes and water-pots,
Invite the ghost of the wood to live there;
Many trees make one shade.

I have heard of the Houses of Parliament of England,
That it is falling down since nobody marked the slabs,
Nobody prayed with the quarry and carried the stones
To their new cliffs the right way up. You should show
    respect!
I daresay the whole panelling is in the wrong way round,
The beams do not flow in the correct direction of the tree,
That the timber-posts are arsie-roofsie, and no person
Has provided house-room for the angry ghosts.
Why, you use conglomerate of wood to print your Hansard,
No wonder the words go all ways in the thick white slab,
No wonder your rulers are confused, in a Chamber crowded
    with shades
And leaves of shadow flaking over their mind in perpetual
    autumn.

Yes, the tree is the house of God,
From which we get warmth and fresh fruit
And a map of our environs. I build a city
Like this tree's spaces, our branches scoop avenues,
Our rafters bud birds in our melody roofs.

THE WOOD TAPES

This oak, recording of two hundred weather-years,
The swift clouds, the thunderstorms, the nutrient floods
Writing on wood. How do I play back?
It is a two-hundred-year second.
It is solid time, breathing.
It photographs the long body of the sun.
It photographs the long body
Of the villagers, of the village.
Dream under the tree
Conceive under the tree
Bear under the tree
Eat under the tree
Be eaten by the roots of the tree
Rise again like a tree
In cursive script

The tree breathes quietly
Like a recording angel
Writing quietly

I take an acorn home
For slow playback,

For genealogy.

EVOLUTION

Shiva-Shakti sweet frog-legs where leaping is in the springs
Up high, higher, high as you can get, the person-springs
Leaping on land, in bed, or standing
In holy mirrors for their intercourse, the statues;

At first that springwater made fishskin for swimming
Like flow in the flow, then for dancing
Upright in the springs as frogs, now

Enclosed the living springs themselves,
Dancing in the woman, in woman-skin,
And dancing in the spring her elf,
Fathered by leaping, leaping of itself.

Crown her with green!
Bring her caves and water to the man of beards.

VERY EARLY AMONG THE ISLANDS

The bees grazing on the young saplings, herds of goats
Barging among the flowers, pollinating them,
The yellow-flanked, sweet-smelling goats;
A basket of frogs' legs still kicking with the vitality in them
Carried across the flood tide by the tall circus-owner
In his icy coat among the early-morning people
Huddled in their shawls rowing over the glittering
Water alive like sunlight on a coffin: the whole boat
Is pure early-morning will to get to work;
They disembark among the smell of herring,
The glitter of scale; she mounts a packing-case,
She picks a fish-scale off her glove and begins to speak.

FIELD-MARSHAL WATER & GENERAL GIN

Learn to speak twittering for the speeded-up ears of the dead;
There are not many powers; there are no warlike powers:

Not even General Gin, washing his hands in the soul,
Waking in a green bottle.

                              I sit on my territory in the rain,
In my cage of water, with its floor of water,
Its white ceiling from which water falls in rods,

I walk among the hollow yarrows, the willows
That take the water, the umbellifers that hold water
In one clear gout high off the ground, in beads like those
The cobweb strings

                              there is the glassy spider
That leaps out to drink up its prey of water;

I sink a glass of it, am as drunk as Adam.

FOR ALL THE SAINTS

My schoolmarm recommended saints
With a tone of sexual secrecy
Like eating something very nice
And I thought of a pallid fellow
Of blancmange curded of mummy's milk
Moulded by acceptance
In vesture saintly suitable
And as we talked of him in sips
Little bites would slipper down
Hardly noticed until he'd gone
And the relics of bones
Left on the sides of plates
(None for politeness or Mr Manners)
A tooth, a lot of hair under the table
A strand plucked off the tongue
And the white eyes sucked
And softly crushed.

69

I met a real saint much later,
It was inside a woman
The saint was very strong
And beat his wings
And resurrected again and again
In smiles and laughter and electric gliding,
I strode into the saintly waters, waves gripped like bone.

A MOVE TO CORNWALL

I must raise a teashop in this place with my own two hands,
I am marrying a wife to conceive a child to adventure
Once more in these mother-lands, these hills
Like great fat mothers in green, dreaming
And as they dream sweating slightly in their sleep;

And the woods of grey oaks unravelling from their age
In green foils and glossy membranes this dawn's freshness;

The black-and-white fungus like a branch of magpie;

The radar we call trees reading the weather day by day,
Building models of the weather vertically in grids
Fining to twigs, the climbing axis of rings,
Cylinder upon cylinder of recorded weather,

Like old people crabbed with their reading,
Cramped among their books, the forking pathways between
    stacks,
Each apple a complete summary indexed in ten pips
That I shall serve baked brown and running in juice
With a core of sugar like melted resin,

With a drawer of money,
With a drawer of forks smelling of fish;

The child runs in from the swings; I gave her scalding hot
    weather-apples.

LIVING IN FALMOUTH

I

Seagull, glittering particle, climbing
Out of the red hill's evening shadow into sunslant
At high tide and sunset; there is a moth
On the rusty table that spreads out wings
Like lichened tombstones.

A crackwillow leaf
Floats into an ashtray; we are among mirrors

And water, and the small windowed boats
Gently in the tide play with long beams
Like silent swordplay

And the gull arrives into the high air
Still full of sunshine, and his particle shines

And the boats knock gently among the shades
And the heads nod

And the good and bad dreams come swimming
Up out of the water glittering as they arrive

Sliding from under the red hills on which
The four-legged phantasms of wool graze,

Cloud-dreams let loose a moment of shower,
Dream-tides knock the fencing dream-boats
And two-legged dreams make one flesh.

II

I sit inside one of her granite tents
Praising against reason the high winds,
The stars hard like gimlets, her bronchitis,
Her onsets of winter and damp moulds,
Her spooks that do not linger,
Her magic touches.

She is only the same town from day to day
In the sense that a book is the same from page to page:
Or her water in the estuaries banked high
With mica-mud that glistens like satin garments
Ready for the spring to put on and shake out
To every colour, is the same water
That lies glowering under corpse-skies.

III

The tourists run like tides through granite houses,
Their ebb the dereliction of seaside pavilions,
Summer woods like smashed clocks, cliffs
Like crumbling cloudscape, dry-rot like wood-spooks
With white cobwebby arms: a bad smell, holding
Out a large repair-bill. Falmouth's bathing-beauties
Are sewing next summer in their dressmaking classes,
Her art-school a tenement of night-dreaming canvasses;
His clouds a tight lid God fastens on the box
Full of thousand-year-old churches and stony boarding-houses
Deciduous of visitors; her echoing mines
Terrible art-galleries for works
Of miner-death that mills tinfoil, of cars in the raw
Bleeding over the roofs of profound caverns. That
Organ-note as the Redruth wind blows over the moor
Winds on the pipes of long-dead mines,

Brings all the bad weather, all the 'flu.
This is the wind that blanches Falmouth, shrinks it
To thin-glassed tombs of drunken landladies;
Her blossoms wither, like an alcoholic flush;
The tourists ebb like tides out of the houses.

IV

Falmouth water like a seven-fingered hand
Flat on the land. We have early elephant,
Bear, ox-ancestor and deer. The deep creeks
Were communication lines between hill forts
Where the hairy matriarchs crept for cover. We escaped
The shunting glaciers that streamed across Europe.
There was a language, part Celtic and part Latin;
A sell-out to the God quartered at Exeter;
A religious college in low woodlands
Near the head of Penryn river; and a chain-boom
Across the creek in the name of St Boudicca.
Until our first-born comes I am an invader.

V

Sun steers from the muddy Falmouth east
And docks above Swanpool, the air clears,
The sun's great hull lies above us, it is time,
Which is a red-hot hull. The great sun-sailors
Take liberty and stroll about the town,
The drawing-rooms expand as they peep in,
The hills are emerald and the cliffs sheer gold.
Their leave is short. They one by one ascend
The shrinking ladders of the dusk
Into the smaller, redder, westering boat. Shall we board
Into the night? To a man we have a ticket.

VI

A ship's figure-head bobbing in on the tide?
A floating pew, shaggy with saints?

Then I saw some of the hair was roots, it was an oak
Upended, a tree swimming ashore.
It bumped against the quay, nobody I could see
Stepped off its felloe of roots, but the town lightened
As if this traveller had tales. Two hundred years
Of voyaging oak, by its girth; say it had sailed
Round the world upsidedown since Garrick cast
An acorn into the Thames from Parliament Bridge. We got a
    tractor
And wrapped chains and lugged it from the harbour,
The gears screamed with the weight of the wet leafhead
Spread through the harbour like a green medusa
Dragged out of the sea full of acorns and foliage
Encaching tons of brine. I think the rains had clawed it
Out of Trelissick's precipitous shores upriver;
The Clerk replanted it in our Gardens. In my dreams
It is a true sea-oak, riding shockhaired over the dark water,
Voyaging through the years white-barked like moonlight,
Its branches like veins of light dredging the deep.

VII

The whole world's water at some time or another
Flows through the Carrick Roads, bringing
Its memories and Chinamen, its Portuguese ships,
Its sectarians and its briny sea-fruit.
Some days the water is bloodstained with trade-battles,
Others it is birth-water running like hot fat,
Sometimes it is industrial dregs, quite often
It runs pure from crystal springs:

And Helford oysters
Sit in the Passages selecting these waters.
Harvested by leathery faces with good eyes
And hands like watercourses, they entrain to London,
To the potted ferns and bow ties,
Where they induce savoury dreams of moonlit water
And Ancient Cornwall, in new young tycoons,
Seductive Poldark dreams that draw the money west . . .

We watch the great cars glide by to the boardrooms,
We own only topsoil, the minerals are reserved,
The ground is sold under our feet.
The Oysters call them here, the Blooms keep them.
They will own everything. Let the land
Packed with underpalaces of gold dripping with oil
Be oyster-tales only, told to a mining penis
On a hotel-bed in London; let it be rumours only, lest all
Our first-born be made miners by the great absent landlords:
Not made deep starved miners by the enormous absent
    landlords.

VIII

The old intelligent villagers, the brilliant old village
Studies at the Open University over the antique wireless in
    the kitchen;
George the Cowman crosses the Tamar to get his degree next
    Tuesday:
He will be a physiologist with cross-fertilisation in economics.
Meg who milks has a doctorate in the Botany of Byres.
Carpenter Joshua studies Geology which is what his trees
    grow from:
How the rock grinds into green wood which planes and
    seasons accurately!
Jack Dustman carries books into the house bin-secretly, and
    reads Bones.
Baker Jones spells out Philosophy in the light of his red ovens.

IX

Cinder-cakes and sour beer. In the cider-cellar,
A corner stuffed with cobwebs, and a little grey drinker.
He drinks and drinks until his loins hurt, and what does he
    see?
It is what he thinks he thinks that matters to him now.
He thinks of all the stars like animals, he thinks he dreams
He snips a piece of bristling fur from each, and puts
Peltry of light into his purse to sew a suit from.

He jerks awake and laughs, in his cider-cellar corner.
When he tries to tell us about it, he gets lost
Among the processions of animals, and animal-headed men,
In among the feet and hooves plashing starlight. Amazed,
I suppose, like him, I love the moist stars of morning:

Orion with his brilliant cock shining like the wet spiderweb,
Like a ladder of light heavier than all the world,
Climbing in his drenched plumage like pulsing snow,
Like a silver beaten so long that it gives back light in pulses,
Or like a black tree over-arching, of white apples with pulsing
    juice,
Or like a rainfall so massive it gluts and cannot fall,
Or like a full-rigged black ship, sailing with all knots white,
Or like wet herringbones at the rim of a great black plate,

Or am I drunk on apples like crushed stars, potent fruit,
That turns you grey and folded one day as cellar spiderweb?

X

Our radio is sensitive, but there is, thank God,
Beethoven sunlight beaming from the ionosphere,

Yet I can hear rain on the radio, and I think I can hear
The sheep tangled on the hillside, and I'm pretty sure
I can hear the broad black stairs of the slate quarry
Like pages torn out of the open hillside
Rustling packets of static;

And there is thunder! far distant,
High-pitched, like cellophane;

The soft grey sacks of rain pass over
In scratchy slippers,
The water is a continual whisper
That paces all ways down out of the skies,
Plashes on boulders, puts itself together
In new ways, raising rain-smells

Over the boulders, down from the moors;
You can hear every rasp and scratch
Of water from our speaker,
Every drop in the whole sky:

And Beethoven's gone, dead
And buried in busy Cornish water.

XI

Sea-waves that are dry
Come off the tide
Or off the rolling Redruth highlands,
Electrical Winds,
Charging us up

It is one explanation.
Waves of exhilaration,
Waves of political rich broadcasts put out by the moorsoil,
Sparkling their invisibilities, recharging us.

The real broadcasters are marching, they are a sightless surf,
There is wave after wave of imperceptible police,
Invisible black psychiatrists in coats the colour of sea-wind,
Invisible white healers in the moonlight
Charging us up

The gusty weather heaves all the leaves of the brain,
The red cells scatter, you can see views through them,
We shall be down to the skulls soon —
Recharge us!

The dead have powerful lungs,
Lungs like parks, sky lungs,
The cemetery sex-adepts at their pursuits,
Joining the worlds with their maggoty electricities,
They set my mind to work with poisoned arrows
That dance you to death like windy trees
Charging about.

From this room we see a clock of breeze
And clouds that run fast or slow depending on
How much we interest each other,
Recharging ourselves

Great dockleaves stampeding in veridian pelts,
Herds of them with muscles of breeze,
Leathery resurrectionists!
The dew crackles and sparks,
Charged up,

In this wind the Goddess kisses every child at once.

XII

The church is very real, absolutely too real,
It is realer than me, realer than where I live;
If this church is a house then I am a white shadow;
Look, there are written stones here 200 years old.
Being my senior by 200 years they do not speak to me,
Except with formal cursive manners like engraved visiting-
    cards
Quoting their names and numbers, their vast antiquity.
They are so still my footsteps must fidget them,
I expect they wish I were as still as they are,
Sitting in some pew studying stoniness until I grow slatey-
    cold.
And there is that vast cross-death that is worshipped inside,
Tainting the air with sweats and hymns so that breath,
Which is something he doesn't need on his side of the altar,
Is like a superfluous whispering of trees, appropriate to trees
Which are best cut down and employed as crosses,
Or chilled till they turn to stone; this death
Is so vast and old that the local deaths are trivial,
The people of the stones have not died, they have moved into
    the yew-shadow,

Which is a tree that has been casting shadows longer than I
    have,
And my parents who cast me are moving into the shadow: I
    follow slowly.

THE FAMOUS GHOST OF ST IVES

A single big drop of water rolls along the back streets,
Along the slim back streets of haunted St Ives;
John Jabez, former mayor, out for a stroll in his town
Walks into the man-sized lens. He thought it was
A constituent rolling the shadows under a street lamp,
Walked up to it with hand out but it is a water-drop
Higher than his hat with in it reflected
The whole of St Ives with harbour intact and himself
Hand-out in the back street his face pulled round.
He leans on the tough skin to get a better picture
And pop he is through being taken for a walk
Like a foetus in a bottle or a sailor in a glass berth,
Breathing safely through his whole skin, thumb-sucking.

'As you rebounded from the rubbery drop
You saw yourself looking out
Like the face of St Ives; what did you see
When you were the ghost's face?' 'I saw with water,'
Says John, 'and I saw water, with men
Like ships sailing on it. Some were great-masters
Strung with confetti-bunting, and some were prison-ships,
And the colourless groans slid over the water;
Others were ships that were jewels
With no people on them; some were crammed to the decks
With good white fish they freighted for others;
Others were ships empty but for the clean satisfaction
Of joiners and sailmakers; one was full
Of hogsheads of wine and crates of communion wafers;
Another was crafted of nothing but

79

Ribs of light and canvas that blew and spoke, and was
    swarming
With happy ghosts, and with a pang

This dissolved in the sea which I saw
Was the hold of a ship with its world-hull of rock
And flowing sails like mansions of cloud,
That shaped its big orbit; then the Drop creamed
And broke up like a wave cresting,
Left me unjointed with joy, my face streaming.

FLORENT

The saliva passed into my parched mouth like a shower,
Like the rain in the clouds, her eyes
Under that ferocious cap had dried all my juices,
But when she spoke and asked me my name, my prick
Sprang forward like the tough head of a turtle.
Nothing about her should have done this,
Skin with great pores, tobacco-plumes up her grey hair,
Sallow lips, jagged teeth and a dress like an overall
Rumpled and roughly tied over a figure like a pillow:
Yet my cock stood stiffly to attention, crowing silently.
She lay back and spread her immense legs, like logs
They seemed to me, but my prick, lantern-
On-a-stick, knew the way; I feared the smell, the depth,
But nothing daunted him, and I was gripped
By corrugations which soon melted my skin and my mind.
I woke with him still inside a lovely black girl,
Slender, with white teeth, red lips and tongue,
A rogue of a girl, alert and smiling. 'Where is . . .?
I asked, she pulled my ear, 'Leave off
That white trash, do you heah?'

STONE FATHERS
(*Scillies*)

Stone is the stone island in the stone-coloured sea
With the stone houses built on it. You see those rounded
    pebbles
That grow to boulders or shrink to gravel on its beach,
That look like eggs; if you split one you would find as meat
The swirling solid inside marked like the embryo of a
    landscape
With a stone sea, and houses, and flint-coloured persons
Not going about their business. To this stone
These houses full of people are empty, are eggshells
Through which a little bad wind blows, and a little
Membranous water that soon boils off its rock. 'Where has
    the future gone?'
It asks, 'where are my descendents?' says this ancestor
Still a stone foetus, 'what happened to the rest of me,
Ground into soil or melted and spurted across strata
To be bedrock and bear the soils that feed the future?
Just these empty shells? Have my descendents left this stone
    planet
In rockets of stone? When stone loosened its grains
For evolution's sake, what rewards?' My father

Steps over the threshold of the seaward cottage, tests the air,
Lights his pipe in the doorway, flings the spent match
He shakes the flame off, over the hedge. He is seventy
And he will have come and gone while this stone blinks its
    eyelid.
Suddenly, the whole beach of stones opens its eyelids,
I can see they stare, they are all eye, the beach glows with
    attention;
They do not see me, in their ranks, like blind Easter Island.

The little islands like headbones through which the sea is
    creaming.

81

EXCREMENTITIOUS HUSK

In the bright light which is the sun's excrement,
That which it throws off in its processes,
I saw the big spider wrestling, intricately involved,
Wrestling with a shadow, with a filmier spider.
Was this its mate that it is sucking dry, is it
Topping up its fertilised eggs, the tight little capsules
With their juice of their father? Oh horror, I said,
That life comes out of death, and that this spider
Is feeding its children on its lover; and I saw
The spider struggle as a man might struggle
Out of his boots and his trousers soaked in the river,
And I saw the spider crooking and uncrooking its knees,
Extricating specks of claws from outworn skin,
Giving birth to itself in fits, like a belly-dancer, and having
    done
Scampering away leaving its dead self stuck to the altar-stone

Of St Cuby in Cornwall, mock-celtic restoration
It had chosen for its transformation
In the rosy light of the phony roundwindow,
With the little stream chugging under that altar
Where the Saint's bones would have been laved to make
    miraculous water
Passing south through his skeleton for every pilgrim to drink
In the fabulous middle-ages where every other bone was a
    saint,
And the spider was a nothing, and the altar too busy to think.

CONSIDERING THE WHITES

I saw a great many black people at the flower-show
Among the bleeding stems of the smiling daffodils
The narcissi of waxy maquillage like cold fried eggs,

Magnolias like pinked claws, and the prim stocks
Like muted energies fastened to old ladies' hats.
Our elm forests may not be much but our geology weighs,
If only I could let you see the geology-show by slicing the
     floor!
Our flowers are echoes of deep strata, twinklings from black
     afar.
It is no matter of underground lava and hot springs
Mud baths and blossoming geysers in tourist parks
But the immense cold crystals of metal that underlie our
     ground
Like the plans of cities outlined in zinc, like cold iron rivers
Leapt by bridges of coal, all slow, and cold, and very
     powerful.
It is these patterns that rise through our soil,
We only drive our roads where the magnetic city draws us,
Our churches stand on nodes of cold shine, and our glass
     laboratories
Patiently behind their lighted skylights work out some
     mineral pattern.
The people fall in urban patterns, like filings in magnetism,
And the hard underground flints reflect like interruptions in
     broadcasts
That have the voice of a snowflake, spread out under the
     counties.
Our geology has crystallised us and bleached us, black people,
Did you ever prefer ours to your rocking continents?
Ours outstares generations and sees family names packed
     underground
Watching the bright planets through the black arms of yews;

Our armorial bearings should be a skeleton and a zinc
     snowflake.

THE SCHOOLBOY AND THE DOCTOR'S BLOT-BOOK
(*Rorschach Test*)

The standing stones with large straight faces,
Large pale late faces, as the quartz
In the granite posts shone back the twilight;
And as the wind hissed in the hanger's leaves
With the throbbing note of the heavy trunks
They were Easter Island turned-down mouths
And eagle noses with closed eyes
Ready suddenly to unlatch
And catch him in their radiance,
And he would be a new stone down which the dew ran,
Not due to open his eyes, being blind stone,
Till he could catch another schoolboy on his own.

The Doctor showed him a book of stains,
He had to say what he saw in them,
He saw heads like bursting stone, and heads with heavy wings,
And a black sun with its rays crooking,
And a black sun for seeing in the dark stone with,
And an invisible man slinking through stained stones,
And he told the Doctor this, who froze like a stone;

And the boy saw the large clear flower towering above the
   house,
A lily of water whose pad was the tarn on the cliff,
And whose stem was his home's white-tumbling brook;
But in the Doctor's book of pictures, it was black.

RESCUE

A cave with a spring, and a library,
Awareness of forms: the nakedness

Of a herring, daft eyes in the sun.
Awareness of danger: white claws

Beneath the white gloves, fists
Made of barbed wire. Knowledge

Of who changes, who washes her mask
Daily in the well, of whose back

Is crooked: look behind you. Knowledge
Of the executive, and of the little men

Of mist, who carry no dust on their feet,
And with that burrowing, desperate head,

Knowledge of psychiatry: the mentally ill
Are incapable of breathing deeply

Booms the Doctor, out of his brass lungs.

SEANCE

Totem-pole, riveted to the wall,
Image of spirit-intercourse,
The creatures of all-living
Surfacing through the long shaft.

A female-male figure formed from this and that.

He stirs the soft water in the copper bowl;
A Lewis Napier rose rests in a human footprint;
The deep red candles preside from the black glass;

There is a crumpled paper message stained with letters and
    spatters!

It is the spiral vestibule to the spirit-world.
They pull paper-faces out of her vagina, endlessly.
There is a horn-and-wood phallus with a pouch of unguent.

There is an imp unfolding from a bolt of cloth.
It makes the client buy the whole story!
The portrait bas-relief in cheesecloth!

She spoons
The fish-eggs so clean and oily, so white,
A concilium of meaty billiard-balls.

It is the best white food for after the seance,
Under the totem, by the tray of dirt
With the spirit foot-print and the ghost-rose
Whose perfumes from its repeated veil stretch breathtaking
    fingers.

TWO VISIONS OF SCIENCE

I

The colourless science-dress, the white coat,
The rimless spectacles like menisci, and a navy
Of weddings launched like new ships with clean sails,
The decks freshly planed and the holds full of dowries
Of silvery science-tools, all the bridegrooms
Dazzling in white dresses and not a bride among them.

The tigerish shoals snap colourless holes in the water;

The moon turns into a single bleached drop.

II

A night spent in a darkened pharmacy said to be haunted,
The bottles gleaming on the walls, the scents of medicine
Hunting out each other's disabilities, like cats
Who wish to mate but keep mum their calls,
Crying with their scented rear-ends only
Which are beautifully cut jar-mouths and their stoppers,
Every wraith labelled, every power in its stiff glass place,
Lacking only a prescriber — and here she comes.
'Are you the Doctor?' 'Yes, I am your Doctress.'

AT THE WITCH MUSEUM

Their great god, a dragon decorated like a church;

Her wand in the dragon's tail,
His tongue in her tail

The child of them both arranging the complex détente,
Screwing the utterance into place, minutely,
Crying 'Back a little! that's it, so I can be born . . .'

The witch's belt hung with black discs, silver discs,
Swivelling and fastened close so that walking
Shows silver slices tilting into black, black slicings,
A belt of moons changing as she walks

And her wand, a bone painted black,
Except where a tiny clenched hand is carved
For riveting high up into the vesicles
That melt the jade into her of Prester Serpent.

87

ROOM OF WAX

The witch pulled the lever and her cellar filled with hot wax,
The mice, the boxes of nails, the live matches,
The well-head, the altar and the human sacrifice:
The girl with the welling heart, and the goat-headed man
With dagger dripping on the return-stroke —
Before they knew it, in a flash-flood
Of hardening wax of bees, caught for ever in the act.

The carpet made of her friend's skin, 'Is it not better
To remember him?' the small pizzle lank and empty.
She would walk over it barefoot, remembering him.
It is like brown suede, we make love on it. On the shelf
The young black cat sat in the jar pickling
A smoky wine: 'If you want to be a witch you must drink it.'
I did, and I am; the cellar door swinging open on the smooth
    wax room,
The secrets running away like water in the blueflare
    blowflame.

MESSAGE TO THE UNWRAPPERS

They peeled off the great waxy leaves
He had been buried in, he was looking
Directly at the unwrappers, but he said
Nothing at first, they thought he was still dead
But then his hair rose slowly as though
The wind were in it, and he said: God came
With his terrible great drum
Through the water, and I was near
To drowning when I saw that, but then
He stopped beating and shook me by the scruff
Of my neck and hurled me up
On this sandy shore in my tuxedo

My pockets full of tropical shells. Some wicked men
Pass straight to the volcano, or sink
To the red part of the rainbow
Where they are consumed; but as for me
There was a person who combed
The tallow of fright out of my hair
And wrapped me in fresh leaves for you; where is he?

THE SNEEZE

The great flint boulders like grounded moons
Sneezing lightning as they strike each other, bounding
Down the fell at nighttime in their own light
That shows the slipping hill on the march like drab platoons;

This happened in another way: he was dressed
Like the village idiot, in an old straw hat
And a jacket too big for him out at the elbows,
He came on us shambling and leering, but then
I knew he was no idiot by the lightning of his sneeze.

This happened in another way: my rival in love died,
I place on the dead chest a platter of snuff piled up
To signify he has no need of breath, and I think
That will keep him down, and if not, we shall be warned.

This happened in another way: that baby sneezed,
'It has its soul!' they cried and began calling
Names over it until it sneezed again: that's the one!
(What causes sneezing? Hungry living does.)

89

A BLACK POWER

He sees the sun black, the bright sea is ink,
All fishes are black and all women except black ones,
All paper is black and all writing not so.
The black fire burns into the white coals,
Cricketers are sweeps and the rooks milky doves,
I smile at a person with black teeth my tongue is white
My shoes polished white and all the mirrors
Are black mirrors and the brides dress for funerals
And the white sea breaks in black spray and in the white
    heaven
The black stars drill through from the black beyond.

ROUGH AND LECHEROUS

The wind blows furiously through the laurel grove,
As the frost twists and shatters there are sparks of ice.
The oaks create the morning-mist that is arranged in shelves,
White sequence of oak-shapes as the dew steams off their
    leaves
In the sweet tinge of first sun like a staining of honey;
But he wants the harsh tastes, he is not a man
Who lives in the steering eyes, in the jelly-globes,
The geographies of coloured images without taste or odour.
That he left his white syrup-of-mushrooms in her
In a meadow glimmering in the moist dust
With white puffballs large as lambs, is recorded
In the memory of his palms, the soles of his feet,
His prick, his scalp. He folded the woods up,
And all the moisture with the sheep and the puffballs,
Folded them very small and passed them through her cunt
Like a painted cloth through a ring, and through his prick
Like a lance into the heart as they made love
In the hot rain that splashed and steamed off

Their bodies-in-spate full of tumbling scree.
The birds mute their white cinders, happily fluting.
Now she cooks eggs on the stove of lava-bricks;
He lifts the Mexican sugar-skull white as a seabird
Out of its red paper, and takes it to her,
With its meaning: I wish to kill you sweetly again;
The frost-crackled horse-mushrooms smoking as the sun
    touches.

PLEASING THE BLACK VICAR

A neck-cramp warned me to accept
The presence beyond the altar, beyond appearances.
I rose and stood at the rail and it seemed
I stood in a fountain of some energy whose light pressure
Rose up through the stone floor and my flesh and pierced
The crown of my head and divided into two wings that fell
    over my spine;
The primaries dragged the floor as I walked back to my place,
The church filled with their rustling as I shook them out
Like many prayer-book pages turned but the church was
    empty,
Save for the sound of those wings. I walked out into the
    sunshine,
I felt the porch carved with apostles comb through these
    wings;
Out in the air I rustled them again, as a tree rustles,
As though my spine had leafed in a century of oak, and as I
    did so
Thoughts turned over in my head like the wind through an
    oak-crown,
The bones of my head turned on their stem. I saw the black
    Vicar,
A Jamaican, hurrying between tombs. I wished to avoid him,
I wanted to learn to fly in solitude, but he waved and shouted:
'I see Behind-the-Altar has given you wings at last!'

91

THREE POEMS MADE OF BONESTONE

I

He was called *The Sun* when he was interred
Wrapped in the manner known as Karast.
An Osiris: every dead person was called an Osiris,
A Sun, and fastened round the throat of the Sun
An amulet of green jasper as the seed of renewal
Planted in the Sun's tomb to ensure its rising.
The Neolithics were the same: green jade;
Axes of green flint in Japan; and the Aztec heart
Of the mummy replaced with an emerald: if you desire
    wealth,
Find it, it is still there among rustling tissue.
Green buried in the manuring dead: as if the next harvest
Would be hard jasper trees haunted by jade birds,
And an army of green axes cutting deep in the glades:
But cored in the earth itself, the very nub thunders
With the molten rock of all rocks: green olivine.

II

She walked into his glass cases under the name of Feldspar;
She sat on his desk and was called Sedimentary,
Arenaceous and Chalcedonic, in the form of a vase
With a watery pattern of coloured bands rising six inches;
She was siliceous and microscopic in the manner of
    Radiolaria,
And he had some fine photographs blown up of her secrets;
But Orthoclase was her favorite form, triclinic;
His bones yearned for her like real stone.

III

The hairy god bristles: the Dog Star pulses
In its bristle, snaps at the heel of the Hunter,
Is the Sun of our sun, the centre our star
Swirls round, and a God of Egypt reputedly,

More likely a Goddess. They would calcine the bones
Of young children into a fine ash if they died at that age,
And they would take the skull of a grandfather, or their
    father,
And they would fit the crown with a base and saw off the
    jaw,
And pack the skull-urn with the child's soft ashes,
Singing songs to Sirius as she rose after Orion;
What has the light of this snapping star
To do with a son crammed back into his father's bones?

ORION PACING

The stars large and wet like snowflakes.
Orion the waterfall hunter.
He searches the ground beneath
For the waterfall in which he can lie down
In which he can replace his reflection
It will pull his stars close together
It will shrink him; the white man climbs out
Of the thundering water, the night-black foam.

Just now he is small silver knuckles. He is little bones,
With dangling prick big as a buckler,
He is like a skinny tree carrying large white apples.
In summer he is born on earth from the river.

He has his photograph in white lines on Cerne Abbas hill
His stars must have been shrinking there in the enormous dew
Then the lightning struck, and outlined him.
This is how he ascends at the end of summer,
He is the lightning that goes up, and the thunder made visible.
He is a thunderflash, caught on the black ceiling.

Rainbows from the Moon hang under the black oak-boughs,
The rain is like a falls, he is wading through it

With a lantern held high above his head, he cannot rest
In this water, it would pull him deep underground.

I am obliged to lie down in the enormous wind,
The suction at the back of its driven clouds,
The wind shakes the big trees, and the wooden house,
And the maids in the garrets like white soft fruit.
Then the sky clears; the merry voices of the Marquis's
        children;
Orion like a full-rigged ship; a town planned like Orion
With a tremendous lighted boulevard at its loins;
Computer-circuits printed like Orion, tied
In bright points which are full of information;
The stars rustling, the wheat twinkling,
White man-splash on velvet, bullets of electricity.

STARSTRUCK

I stare at the sky and try to make my eyes
Bigger and blacker than the lenses of telescopes,
Deeper and sharper than the eyes of hares;
Look! Betelgeuse has a grain in its redness, like jam-seed,
And Sirius shines like bright drifts of lemonade
That suddenly stain with a fresh tide of red.
Orion's lean figure has stepped over the skyrim threshold,
No longer composed of dots, but interactions and centres.
I will draw him down so that he occupies my limbs
With his yellow dog snapping red at my heels;
I will be coated inside with these immense star-glutens,
So that my faults are mere details in the immense glowing
        picture,
So that I become visible while whistling in the dark bedroom,
And paint glowing pictures on your inside red walls,
On the crystalline bedroom interiors between your two big
        toes.
I stare at Orion so hard he is tattooed on my tongue;

I say Orion Orion Orion very rapidly and softly
My tongue wrapping round like a telescope of many
    utterances fitting together.

YELLOWBACKED AND BUTTERHEARTED

I

The child's heart, turned to gold
Found glittering at the bottom of the rain-butt
By the sunshine beating in its stouted sides.
A rainwater butt still turns my heart to gold.

Water and wood carried into the cellar, by sunburnt men.
The torturers follow, with their screaming bags of tools,
Whose preference is iron to bone
Chiselling out a confession on the skeleton,

They are pale, but smell like smiths
As they survey the raw material of screams.
They fill me from the butt, with leather buckets,
Their job is to pass my life in front of me
With a funnel-through-the-teeth drowning-technique
Until I say 'That is when! Now I can tell all.'

I see my heart of gold glittering in rainwater,
I dive back into cowardice for it, and love my tormentor.
The yellow button hops away, croaking.
The gathered rain tastes salt as butter.

II

My noblewoman's face is clean, my body the flogged
    scoundrel.
I have personal servants to sponge my lips,

My body is the torturer's: privilege of rank.
My ear owns a priest, whispering like a private chapel.

The limestone-tasting unity of the glass of cold water.

A painted scourge, or disciplinarian of teak.
A sjambok with silver barbs starring the tresses.
Silver drinks blood; the noblewoman is drained of it.
My commoner's body
Turns on its tits, the priest whispers, and silver
Melts through my back like the unseen constellation Scourge.

CHRISTMAS AT BAD MANOR

The Passion carved in bone,
Bad thoughts like large dead flies
Upright in all the choir stalls
Rustling like starched surplices
Light as great salt leaves,
Heads together, swishing their hymnbooks,
Skeletons in the web.

I wear a flesh-coloured jacket
Buttoned with glass eyes,
Obedient to the priest, get married.
There is a cradle 150 years old;
The great grandson inspects it for worm.
Silver hands were hammered for the bride's gloves.

The bridegroom opens an 18th century hutch and pours
    brandy,
The cards pattering on the greenbaize table,
The snowflakes outside lying still in the evergreen sorting-
office,
And a two storey Christmas-tree snowed up with father's
    white parcels.

BLANK INSIDES

'We will be glorified after death,' the promises said.
The skeleton rubbed with bicycle oil for glory.
These owls seem like winged skulls stooping.
Are souls meteorites of bones the angels kindly take up
In their starlit hands to beyond the stratosphere,
Raise them above their haloes and drop them sheer
To be glorified in the streak of re-entry fire?
Or the stone cadaver of the glorified poet
Carved on his tomb with both hands on his Shakespeare?
His insides are blank, see with a sledgehammer.
I walk through the glorified church itself
Under the rose along its hollow gut
Through its blank insides up to the table-stone
That turns food into flesh. How I prefer
The console ridden by its million-digited master,
The door into the organ like Another Church
Of silver birchgroves, singing within this stone.

THE NINETY-TWO DEMONS

The vast brown shallows planted with seaweed
Awaiting harvest: iodine harvest, the violet element,
Evening element of the violet clouds vast as the shallows,
Vast languid harvest beating in the rock-pools.
The seaweed-scyther comes, his trousers rolled,
His hands crackled with salt sea-gathering, the little rivers
Of hand-blood add to the millions-of-brown-tongues harvest
Licking salt, licking blood from the gathering hands.
The boulders flower slowly with stone barnacles
Built of boulders that long ago dissolved in sea-chafe,
The dissolved ancient boulders rebuild on the boulders.
There are only ninety-two elements and most of them come
    from rock,

And the violet iodine returns like hair to grow on the rock,
And the human feet made of seawater and stones
Splash in the shallows gathering iodine
Under the violet clouds, among the dissolving rock
Made of the ninety-two demons of existence who
Travel the length and breadth of it, whose names
Enable you to chemist them; you are they.

SUPERSTITION

Crown the boundary-stones with garlands;
Never swear within the hearing of your bees;
The clouds themselves like white beehives listening.
You swear; the rain falls like glass bees in a swarm
Humming with their speed, each one smelling of flowers,
Many flowers. Flat sheets of flowery cloud
Rise off the river-meadows, enrolled above.
The gorse-reeking cliffs give off jagged cloud;
The exact shape of Beeny in cloud-cast rises
Again and again in sequent shapes of scent,
The cloud-flower born of flowers in a flower-shape at flower-
    time.
If I approached the hive with scented lotion on my hair
They would scream in concert and launch their stabbers.
The other world comes through with a certain note
Which may be a perfume. It looks like this world,
But not at first. It comes through
Like a sound which is the sky or a perfume looking like
Bees swarming or a certain saying. Sometimes like hell:
The cliff begins to chatter and big flakes of slate fall,
The house sings so hard it burns, the hillside
Sits back opulent in its exposed iron-veins, the house
Settles shivering as though its walls were rushes,
The air is thickly brackened with invisible structures,
And the roots of this house are mingling with the roots

98

Of all the other houses beneath the pavements and my legs
    dream
They are cellars packed with roots lapping from burst
    barrels.
Some of the ancient gods have become illnesses;
Others trail invisible odours like embroidered mantles;
Then the stone cliff looks opulent, like pyramids,
The cliff looks seated, like the king of schists;
Out of this valley they dug our houses, in the quarry
We move through their walls like corridors, are stopped
Only by solid rooms still packed with seated kings.

CLOCK OF CLOCKS

I

Toothed wheels, the dust ringing
With tock, belfry of clappers
With high long tones, like tears,
With skirts that cry intolerably
And wheels packed between four corners
Of stone whose inner crystals
Take o'clock's shape. I tie it
To my wrist, I pocket it, the case
Ringing like the tiles, the rafters,
A church on my wrist, a box of hours.
Who do I meet in this crowded
Church, with the pews meshing
And the greasy altar with a wheel hanging
And the rose-windows that connect
And the doorway like a toothed almond?
Is it a gymnasium, with forfeit mincers?
Is it a tree of steel I am in, or a smithy
Full of anvils arranged on wheels
That beat with hammer-blows, or a stable

Full of chariot-wheels that cannot stop fighting,
And clockwork hooves galloping,
Of empty goods-trains running on time?

II

The clock of oil, through which
The shocks run in shadows;
The clock of wood, from which the fruit
Drop every second; the Chinese wooden
Water-clock which fills a mill
Swarming with woodlice like cunningly jointed
Bracelet wrist-watches with legs;
The sun-house clock
Of revealed architecture through whose spaces
Shadows and lighted areas fall, creating
Rooms, cabinets and clocks, staircases,
And deleting them as the day passes, containing
The cobweb-clock that has eight hands
And jaws and feeds on motes; the two-door clock
That sends rains in the hands of a young girl
Holding cat o' nine-tails of silver chain,
Or sunny weather like a man
With a painted torch-bulb for a face;
The unfrocked priest says mass
In the roofless clock, under the diamond points
Of the clock of lights whose teeth are suns;
On the marble mantelpiece the flint clock
Strikes sparks every second of the day and night,
Invisible by sunlight, whose pillared halls
Crackle with earth-fire, the true time.

III

The clock of meals, toothed wheels
With soft lips, eat
And time stops; the clock of sex,
That galloping timepiece; the clock
In the burning house that ticks on

100

Until it melts; the clock of cogged soot
In the hooded smoke of bonfires burning seconds
That drop from rusty clocks striking Autumn;
The blood-clock of a scarlet ape that bleeds
Exactly at new moon on the temple straw;
The white snow-clock-hat that fits the mountains;
The joke that is a well-timed clock; the clock
That is an oak-tree dripping with water-seconds,
Bright ticks of water; and
The clocks made of money, the clock-exchange;
The clock of shoals of fish under the moon
And wooden fishing-boats with the trawls out
At the right tide to pull up the silver
Loads of time under the moon, which is a blank clock-face
That has sent its hands to sweep the tides; the hand-written
Clock-face of a summons; the clock
Of aid-to-the-poor; the Arts Council
Like a clock with pockets and in them wallets
And when it chimes, notes slide out of the pockets;
The clock of grannie's lace that dishevels
In the tomb that undoes all her knots;
The clock of a man counting his billion seconds
Each one of which is as red as corpuscles;

And the clock of clocks itself, once
Passed through like a hoop, once back.

A GALACTIC TALE

The stiff and foaming milk in the deserted dairy,
The cheesy rafts and crusts, the lactic stench,
The curds in whey like exhaust in summer air,
The quiet shelves of phosphorescent cheese:
Who has deserted milk? The professionals!
The deserted bottles line the streets like soldiers
In platoons that are ghostly emptied of flesh,

The wire shapes of phantom milk stack the floats.
They are swimming in the sea, the creamerers;
The cheesewrights, they are washing off the milk
In the phosphorescent night sea biting as gin.
The windows of the locked dairies shine at night
From the still and souring vats of milk,
The mildews blaze on fluorescent cheeses.
The green milk-mould has got the milk-maid;
She moulders by the green cows she was milking;
The creameries shine with green beams and blue carpets
Like television light that does not flicker,
Like walking on hushed pile glowing like the cinema.
Children of fungus spring out of the green vats,
Sprint out into the milky moonlight and play
In the green shine, puffing clouds of spores.
The military turn their searchlights like the sun,
And prang their projectiles, the big silver sticks
And ravening metal-hided beasts; but the torn children
Explode in more spores that spread more children
Who feed on anything, rejoice in anything,
Rejoice on soldiers, feast on soldiers.

The red-tabbed general claps his mouldy brow.

DEEP-GUIDE BOOK

The ship rotting around its ballast
Of water-worn boulders. The plain bones
Laid to rest in a diagonal gash in the wall;
The course of bricks, each one
Recording the quality of three minutes
In the life of an ancient builder;
The tiny stone chapel with the pock-marked doors;
And, south of the palace gardens, the deep water-churches.

We have underwater groinings through which the swimmer
    slips,
Our worshippers enter the cathedral and stay
And pray in the nave while God beats his drum
In their drowning heads, then they drop
Their stone prayer-books and leap
Past the hurrying gargoyles up through the steeple
And surface to their confessors at its missing tip:
This well with the parapet carved into benches here.
We have surprising chutes signed with a mandala
Which means rebirth through water, and there are bones
In plenty down there that could not leave hold
Of their stone pages. There are canals
And liturgical locks cogged with the calendar,
And in the tidal crypt the moon-saliva heaves.
It was the sainted diver who founded us,
Deep in the flooded graveyard rebuilt foundations
Among the suppurations and rafts of fatty pus
Waving like stinking ghosts out of the drowned vaults.
He propped up the first church; we flooded it
To emulate his feats. Our confessions
Are given in the alligator's lair,
Our deep Bishops are sharks and angel-fish.

DRUID MELODIES

A little book of dead druid melodies,
The stag represents the bush-soul of Christ,
The dead hover behind the masks of that season,
The dog renders him good service with that sensitive nose.
In the cathedral the great rose window
Is made with all the tissues of Christ's body
Living through centuries in pain with the light shining
    through,
Never-dying, the rinse of light keeping the round body alive;
After two centuries his song to light and thin panes began,

The breeze casting dust on his exquisite places;
He is the grafted Man of this cathedral,
Each one selects a Christ to transmit light through pain,
His supersonic cries add their burden to our services,
One immense rose-red window; and here
There are two lovers spread out in this manner, layer over
    layer,
Blood touching blood for decades in a pang
Which the cathedral bells are cast to make audible in a lower
    octave.
These Christs do not have bones, the bones are extruded,
They have the window and the light, of their bones we make
    candlesticks.
Here is a picture of the patroness, with the tongue of her
    lapdog
Cleaning a model of the cathedral carved out of a bone.

FROM THE BATHYSCAPHE

The water has the ragged sleeves of Sandow.
It is far stronger, out of glaciers
It can slide mountains parting with white screams,
Bobbing off in slow motion that takes years.
It flattens the fish: some haunt a living
In the great abyss little better than jellies,
A tentativeness arranged around water in water
That has the pressure of steel, and those
That are not jellies are wafers,
Fining to nothing edge on, suddenly a face.

And it is a drop on the hand-back
Like an eye opening there, or a mouth
Of water suddenly speaking on a stone

Out of a towering sky
Where water has no weight, apparently,

And floats like white aeroplanes,
But aeroplanes are heavy
And this thunder-anvil is heavy as St Paul's
And looks like St Paul's flying to heaven
Whitewashed and full of stainless figures:

How it darkens! and thunder utters
From its open doors, and a towering drop
Strikes the hand-back;

And at the waterfall I consider Sandow's rock-sculpture,
He has made it with his fingers covered in white sleeves
In the laboratory made of shattering vessels which heal,
In the tinkling studio of the waterfall, among fluids and
    music,
With flakes that fall in the hard cold like steel chiming.

SILICON STARS
(*Diatomaceous plankton*)

In the deep of the sea, a dandruff of plankton.
In the thin sunlit layers life thrives,

As it drops into the ever-night of the depths
Buries itself in itself, in fine dust
Always-raining. Adam, look at it

With the eye that God gave you for naming the smallest.
Those are footprints of life sharp as spur-rowels,
They are silicon stars like transparent iron,

Each is a vessel growing from its own centre
And pierced with windows like Washington
And, falling empty suddenly, so raining
Like a snowfall of glass;
                              much whale-meat masters

105

The open ocean, whistling and plunging,
Whose turds of plankton are entirely
The massed crystal vases of the almost-invisible creatures

Hurtling down to line the ocean with mud that is fine
  porcelain.

MEETING AMERICA AT WISTMAN'S MANOR

I

In the house called 'Silver-Springs'
Will the American find what he has rented
In the bedroom, or in the water-gardens? He has brought
  with him
The blue pointers, the real man-eaters;
His children look terrible, with their Colgate degrees,
Their bow ties, their glassed-in eyes,
Their beaufrog faces, their flashy flyboy spectacles.

II

To the beetles in the woodwork, who are sleepless,
We slip in and out of the flaws of clockwork,
We step in and out of the white sound of the clock.
We hang our white heart on the wall and obey its tick;
We do not fuck by the noontide shadow dwindling,
We do not rise by the moon as the loving creatures do,
(The steel-blue flies
Click over the carcass
Like winged black grease that roasts it bare.
I count the bullet-heads, their joints,
There is a month of joints on each fly,
Each is an egg-calendar and full of itself
Which is packed like greasy wheat in sallow pouches.)

106

III

The swans, the wind they tread
Creaks in their clothing, in Vee-formation
They save fat, in the leader's slipstream:
Fly high with the wind, low against it,
Knowing without knowledge the wind's abrasions.

IV

He props an oak-twig on his music-stand
And plays its scutcheoned scars; it has music
That is a score for stripped skeletons;
It has the blood-tree sonata;
It has the last trump.

V

The wind pours by in its pattern and its grain
The forests and the twigs print their wind-shadows
Like fingers trailing in a stream. This soi-disant Scot
Is dressed in a map of the heath he calls his tweeds,
The breeze dressed in an abstract, scented, of the briars.

VI

She has a complicated switchgear
Of buttons and openings and collar-flaps
All down her front of flounces.
I wish she would switch on the plunge
Among the vile stars of rusty barbed-wire strands.

VII

The water scrabbles from the springs
Like silver crabs; the ceiling-rafters
Stretch like braided serpents entranced by firelight,
Like veins tautened by wooden flow.
The house is called 'Silver Springs'.

107

Coming home, the car slides the valley-trees
Back into their heat-haze like plum-bloom;
Up here it is cool. The wood fire
Roasts resins out of the rafters, very slow;
It is this they pay for, the slowness.
The American declares: 'Our expensive Springs
Must be the beds': the grounds have gone dry.'
He points his camera at the sun and it explodes in his hands.

VIII

He should watch Wistman's Wood.
It is like lichen among broken steps.
The steps are colossal; the oaks all crabbed
One way, and combed, the colour of cobweb
Which is clockwork. You can step in its slits
Where the light slices, the cogs twitch,
You are gone.

IX

Time is an English oak.
The meaning of it is a grey acorn.
It spins on the polished table, rolls to rest.
Put it back, dear Sir, put it back.
It is all that is made.
I love your English tales.
Time's beard is green again after April showers.
Time has a human heart
In ribs of wood, a stiff lichen face.
Bang bang bang goes the great Athenian knocker.
He wants his nut.

X

The oak goes through the house and up the oak stairs,
Lays down its foliage-heads in all the beds,
Penetrates the taps that pour out leaves,
Rustles in all the wireless-sets; its canopies

108

Press flat against the bathroom ceiling and construct the true
Lavatree or Pot-plant; we wander through
Its crocodilian pillars, we have lost our rooms,
The panellings grow starred with buds, the floors
Roughen with their barks, we part
With green hands the leafy doors that cannot be locked.
Give him his acorn, Sir, his stolen fruit.
You have taken just one
Nut too many from the English soil. You are lucky:
An oak walks away quietly through the water-gardens,
Pulling its leaf-head free of our swishing windows.

XI

I know the butter of the female
Among the nice slate tombs, wafer-thin,
Black to the north, south-greened;
As we stroll southward, the graveyard vanishes
Camouflaged into its turfy pads.
Her blouse flashing and creasing like bonfires
There is a small rent from barbed wire,
A royalty from rusty stars, a dividend from armaments.
I have met America, and have money, if nothing else.
Money and aggression; now I must marry her,
Marry and disappear.

SPACESHIP AUTOMOBILE

He shrugs on his great car-suit and speeds away.
Another mineral being draws up, and the spirit
Leaves its corpse in the form of a young woman
The shell neatly parked as she glides up steps
And flitting from eye to eye resurrects the house,
Turns its lights on and draws its lids.
I am a ghost in this machine, it accelerates me
Because of its great capacities, its mineral flame

Burns among metals as I put my foot down and it snarls
At its mirror-images polished like glass passing the other way:
I am one of its provisional brains, I am thrown
Loosely free cracking its glass cranium with my own
And the brain within the brain flops free,
Its petrol mingling with mine until a spark
Kindles us and we turn into a black smoke person
Who strides in billions of mineral cells like soft sand,
Like birds of soft soot surveying the whole world, dissolving
  in air.
It has climbed its way out of the precipitous ores coloured
  like vineyards,
It has passed through the fires like flower-nurseries,
Now it has earned its soul, its population of souls
That air it as though the city had burst its veins,
Flowing through the dusky thoroughfares in car-light.

The cars live us now. What is the meme,
The gamete of the machine, how did its great code
Of metallic genes enter us and guide us
To stamp it out of the earth-marrow? Did some smoke of
  metal
Penetrate the nostrils of the engineer immaculately,
In his pregnant invention swell to a steel foetus?
Our appetite is dressing in earth-machines,
Mineral suits like wombs of mother earth in which we
Hang suspended in our straps at even temperatures,
While the cars, great-eyed, glide on their ways.
We are bottled persons. Car-needs
Created computers; we are no more than mothers'-arms
Teaching the metal to take its first wheeled steps.
The computer soon will be able to move
The necessary motes through the roadlike circuitry
Within the metal hull of the planet
Travelling by radar on its spacious orbit,
Turned entire into car-forms like a stinking garden
Thick with metal flowers and their radio roots
Deep in soil that is circuitry,
That hums with its motion grazing on space-textures,

Like some Rolls-Royce steeped in its own excellence
That has dispensed with his Lordship, her Ladyship,
And, the sun and the moon shining in its coachwork,
Spins though brilliant space with only its clock ticking.

RADIO

The sea foamed crackling blue as the lightning struck it
An immense black lily, the thunderhulk with a stem of
    electricity
Fat as a city block, its roots embedded in water
And branching beneath it in the fathoms and boiling them
With the blue of bolting eyes, blue bolting horses.
All night, like Cockaigne, the surf washed up cooked fish
Good to eat, falling off its bones, and more where that came
    from,
Crumbs from the thunder's table. Out of Hiroshima
The savour of cooked meat arose, a masterpiece
Of military cuisine, enough to feed ten armies,
And poisoned shoals that kill trawlers with radio;
This the radio tells me. And if you packed
The History of Broadcasting into one ten-seconds,
That would fry England, like an immense fish, loose on its
    bones.

ACTING EARTH

Teak ark of menagerie,
Dangerous cabinet of snappers,
Frosted aquarium labelled eels — high tension!

Sliced mother-of-pearl showcase
Hiding its germanium gardens,

Its zoology of striped currents,
Its parklands flowering with electricity,
Its mineral collection that watches everybody,

Its apparatus converting electricity to drama,
Its infusorium of actors and people
Where metal chippings speak with cultivated voices.

Television suicide: smash your fist into the battle
Booming over the waxen window; if you wish to die
Pluck opium from the poppy-field, work your fingers
In the heroin-scene behind the announcer's shoulder:

Otherwise do not intervene
In the designs of the electric toymaker.

We are spread by his skill into a thin layer over the Earth:
Our eyes are set in a mousehole
To watch the polished toecaps mount their stairs
To the granny-murder in the American bedroom;
In a fly-specked lightbulb swings
Our visual cortex over a seedy room
Where the man in a vacant revolver-holster and a torn shirt
Sways from his beating;
We stare out of the lidless shirtfront
Of the drinking-booth waiter across the tumblers of alcohol
On the hurrying tray at the polished black gangsters;
Often we are the gun-sight that lays its cross
Baptising the domed brow of the doomed leader;
Our hands pressed to our face we are the bedside clock;
Everywhere there are flying cameras like aviators or gnats,

In the confessionals, in the pews, at the execution,
At the conception, beware everyone:
Above any object at all a small red light may go on,
And you are on-camera, the Producer is watching.

Out of the deep earth we grew, out of those rock-eaters,
The great trees that nourished us, out of Eden, leaving

Deep under our feet the mineral creation.
What is it to them, that they urgently seek us
To become our machines, to become our wheels,
To transmit our images, to flicker with our passions,
To imitate people, so badly, or actors, all evening?

DIAMOND DAY

The diamonds when they are blue clay,
The colour of corpses, die easily
At the beginning of their career, but later on
They are almost eternal. Only certain carbon is suitable.
In the blue pipe, this Cullinan Diamond was formed
From an entire mammoth that lurched into the volcano:
See all those tusks and hair reduced in a flare
To a few ounces of glittering soul. Is the mammoth
Happy in the diamond? It is mammoth-heaven
Within that diamond and we cannot get there,
Except by jumping into a volcano if we have the call,
But then geology might not choose us, and we wouldn't
    know
Until we woke up in the diamond's eye:
Millions of years have passed. Kafka's novels,
With interminable delays and anonymous powers
Describe earth science on behalf of Prague City,
Which was and is stone wishing to become diamond,
Having collected enough carbon-based life indoors,
But it is half-paralysed with cutting and fitting;
Every block cut, every facade, loses its memory.
America's intrigue was to fuse diamond in the atomic flash:
Populations participate, provide pure carbon.
Now spy on your Parents, look deep and turn the facets:
There is the Mammoth, father of his own soul,
Long-haired sage in a condition of sexual arousal,
As he looked as he dove into the hot rock of rebirth.
(But will she stand, as the city goes up, a diamond?)

DEATH-DREAMER
(Cerne Abbas)

On the plain a frost-flower
Grows big as a city,
The shadows of congregations
Linger in its white churches
Freezing to the walls, layer upon layer,
The people grow whiter. It is a death-dream,
I lie on my sickbed
Like clothes in soak
Who shall unpeel the thick shadows?
The earth grows delved
Porous as bathstone, the big cliffs
Sinter into grave cities;
Earth will pumice us to the bone.
Somebody's lovely Christ
Spins through heaven on thin golden wheels;
The deer have gone, that were
Like running flowers
Of musk in the twilight;

The caves are all lined
With long grass, it blows
In all the sinters,
It fiddles
Like a field of force;
Death comes, she is grassy,

She is too complicated,
She is in many dimensions,
I must simplify myself,
Walls fall away, and fall away on walls
That are falling, she wades
Through the long grass
Clothed in a dress of green movements
But then

114

She simplifies, like the Chalk Giant
Cut in lanes which are its body on the hill of grass;
She is a lamp-post shedding still light
At the left out-stretched heel of the Giant

As at the opening of a pathway cut out of chalk

Or as the woman's hard bones ease to make way.

MATCHES AND BACCY

He cut off the head of the fire,
He tore off its fingers,
He shut its dead fingers into drawer-boxes;
The head went on flaming
Under the belling chimney-shadow;
I stare in it for oracles;
I draw on a clay pipe,
Soothed, I see sooth,
My tranquillity breeds oracles;
The fire-skinned Indian
Marks the tobacco-store,
I smoke his head,
I look into my pipe,
It is a stone tent, in its doorway
A peaceable Red Indian glows
And dims, doing his breathing,
Feeding me magic which is poison.

THE SCIENTIST AND HIS WIFE
FLY ON THEIR FEATHER-MATTRESS

The kind young researcher smelling of death,
With his young wife; the youngish physiologist,
The smell of the rats he has tormented to death
All day in his laboratory that clings to him
And excites his wife and troubles his dog . . .
The bright eyes multiplied in the bottle-rows,
The bright claws scratching through his labyrinths.

All the little fishes are the genitals of Osiris;
All the little mice are the consort of the Goddess.
The God explodes himself in swarms of rats and mice,
He sleeps dismembered below the water in his shoals.
God shall be tormented in his fishes and mice,
Goddess shall mourn and rejoice over her fishes and mice,

The long white coat invisibly written with ancient scriptures,

And the wife getting the core of it, the sex of death,
Among their soft experiments in the goose-feather laboratory.

THE PHILOSOPHERS

When we see that cloud enter the sky
We know that God is there; when we see it now
We know it is the same cloud as before,
Though after, none can describe it.
There is a clock timing a time that manifests
In mirrors, with hands pointing to
Mirror-time, and then merely
When it chimes, and suddenly appears,
Or is it only then that I notice it, or time?
It is the china clock, among others,

116

With the gold hands, that moves sideways when I turn
Abruptly as it chimes, perhaps crab-time. The chief
Of philosophers, he I could admire, of certainty
He'd have a white beard, and he'd sit by fire.
He and his school most of their lives
Would sit in reverie by the fire, making up
Philosophy out of the flames, and setting nothing
To paper, lest it scorch. In troubled times
They'd lead the folk and light their torches for them
And teach them arson, so that the Monster
Or the Chancellery will burn, for where
There is flame there is reverie, warm musing
Wrapped in one's grey beard, in holy sandals,
And all books burnt. By thought-compression
One might invent cubical fire, and gelignite.
One sees right down to excited atoms, in a fire,
And people are made of atoms, whence comes
Personal warmth, and love between nations. I linger
By the kitchen fire, which to philosophers
Is the souls of departed cooks, and this is why
The old ranges cook best, being staffed
By experienced souls (though the housekeepers
Of priests after their death are turned to horses
Which keep the glebe-grass short); oh
Philosophers have fearless traffic with ghosts,
Inexhaustible nourishment. The beehive intones
And from that tone comes honey to the mouth,
Sweet as flames are to the eyes, the tawny fire
Of bees, sweetness and the whispering cell-light
Of beeswax candles as though pages
Were rustled in the flame. Will I live
To watch such a master's coffin walk?
Did I laugh like he would at the mutinous donkey
That loosed a steaming pile during the Cornish Mystery
As Jesus died, high up, in his blood-fire? The dung
Smoked like my master's camp-fire in the breeze of frost
That crackled each apple with a lacquer of clear ice,

The opposite of fire — laugh hard at it, all winter!

PEACHWARE

On the stoneware platter, a peach of bloom
Faintly blushing, arse-cleft like a wet dream,
With a gathered-in feeling under the down
Of heavy sap, like a great drop of honey
Held by its fibre and a little napped pelt; at its side
A silver knife with a white bone handle and writing
Cursive on the silver, the surname, Box;
And on the one-hundred-year-old planks
Glossy with beeswax and a hundred thousand man-hours
Polishing, done in peachwood with mountings of silver
At butt and tip, with a bunch of thongs
Riveted with thin stars in stainless steel,
A whip in peachwood, a wicked little whip.

AMONG THE WHIPS AND THE MUD BATHS

She offered the liqueur glass of Grenadine
Between her legs; the beard lapped it up;
She swooned, recovered, said
M. Grenadine's the man for me; and from that day
The establishment was known as Mme. Grenadine's.
I saw her lose her temper with a punter once.
It was unprofessional, but after forty years of coaxing old
        cocks
She thought she had a flier, and it was not.
She screamed at him so furiously the sparks of anger
Danced in her teeth, picking them; she had a mouth
Of blue flame; I *think* I saw this; I was so respectful
That when she blew her top like Krakatoa I saw things
I did not believe. This went with the rumours of China,
How she was said to have learned to ease the slow blue
        lightning
Out of her skin and out of her lover's skin

So that they were sheathed in radiance, and the dark room
Flickered with their body-prints, like sand-dunes electrified
After a dry day. I did go in without knocking once
And I saw something gleaming, but it was so faint,
A kind of mouldy shine on the snoring bodies
Wrapped like beached tunny in their silken sheets.

I have flickered static out of the great bed
Its sheets clung to me and would not be smoothed,
And there is continual restless bedmaking in this place, but
    aside from that
Her power makes me see things, I mean her personality,
    I mean my love,
Among the balustrades and carved galleries of her house,
The damasks and the fur rugs, the whips and the mud baths:

All that sex populates my imagination and makes me happy.

A VISIT TO NETHER POWERS

We stayed with Mrs Frohl, of the crescent smile.
Yes, she with the spider candelabrum on the centre-board,
Creamy tapers flaming up from eight bent joints.
I remember the hen-cries of the babies, the cries of cats
Like babies calling for babies; and crusty rolls
Baked in ranks like tawny skulls,
Their crackled sutures, their flaking domes,
Their fullness of warm white wheaten brains.

It was after the clay-tasting, and the stewards
Had picked up all the bones out of the collapsed dresses
And counted them aloud. I had some experiences:
First I saw an air-girl with rain-bones standing
By the elm-tree with gnats stitching her smile.
Then she went, and I felt the first star's
Tendril brush my face. There were abundant primroses

119

That arranged into the figure of a small prophet of flowers
Lying back in the green grass, preaching at ease;
Beyond the copse the lights of the town,
As the stars did above, made a bundle of white thorns
And I could not tell the stars from our town's horizon.

Now the rain started in earnest and I needed a drenching;
Through my skin I experienced thunder of four colours.
Nearby, cropping the flower-prophet, a sheep's fleece
Stood on end and crackled with the lightning,
And on the mountain in the storm a thousand sheep-fires
Were burning harmless — four-legged fire

With sweet mowing-breath imperturbable.

THE WEDDINGS AT NETHER POWERS

I

The grass-sipping Harvestmen, smelling
Like haylofts on stilts, creaking
Like wet leather; a raven hops
And picks at them through the gravel:
It has macabre dandruff.
In its spotted froth the bark-faced toad squats
Among the daffodils like Stars of David.

II

A wasp crawls over the crucifix, sting out
Searching for a vulnerable part; the savage vicar
Strikes, the usurper bursts in melted butter
And horn-slices; another takes its place
Searching with its sting out over the holy places.

III

A gold-and-black body pinned to a matchstick cross,
The extra leg-pair free, glossy with wax, their cloven
Dancing-pumps shadow-boxing with slow death;
The sting stretched out in agony and clear drops
Slipping along the horny rapier to the tip
Where a woman crops the venom in an acorn-cup.

IV

The laboratory with skylights, the glass assemblies,
Tubes, taps, globes, condensers, flasks and super-hot flames:
With windows wide open to the pouring waterfall
White with every colour and exclaiming with every word,
With roof wide open to the starfall; just down the stream
The Mud Shop, with fifty-seven varieties of bath.

V

Two birds singing together like learned doctors;
The dew is open on every page;
He washes the dog's feet gently with warm water;
She spreads luminous marmalade on cindered toast;
There is no tree of flies in which creamy skulls lodge,
      humming,
No dogs here have intercourse with any virgins;
There is a slug in the garden grey as a city kerbstone;
There is a cool sweet book of one page bound in appleskin.

VI

One hundred ship-weddings, the scoured planking, the pure
      sails,
The bride's train blazing across the scrubbed poop,
The century of marriages and a hundred brides
Pulled over the water by their blinding veils.

121

FOUR TALL TALES

I

The one note all the leaves make as the rain runs over them,
The leaf-note that winds into the deep sough of the trunk
That unwinds along all the root-tapers, down into the atom.
We climbed the lane, and beyond a gate were three trees
Light in their foam of spring leaves, the branching
Slender in the new growth and the first lime-blossom,
And they were as full of bees as they were of leaves,
They were like stalked hives from which the light hum
Of cupping of air hundreds of times a second
In the beeswings glittering with wax under the new leaves
Glittering with their wax, rose like the sound
That planets, captured by the branching canopies
Of lights and ethers, call out down the corridors
They sweep out round the sun-tree, down to each singing
    atom.

II

During the high tides the streams run amber from the peat;
In the Drumming Well the beats grow quick; the lovers
Yawn happily together; the wind brisks and, blowing
Over the church-tower, its scents are sculpted into patterns:
The gargoyled church rips out a wind-corridor,
A furling tunnel like a stocking in which he-shapes
Mingle with she-shadows of air in the lee of the tower
Where the preaching-cross is. In ancient times,
In other countries, minutely-carved stones for telling stories:
The teller's practised voice deciphered the epic
As his fingers rolled the stone: the wind's fingers
Roll this church-stone and we stand in the mouth of the
    story.

III

The butch girl bloused like a shimmering custard
Who helps in the kitchen, hands me a small packet
Of thirty yellow flames; she is the apple-smelling flower-show
  visitor
Dressed in flower prints, who photographs the prizes;
But she wears her cursing-lipstick and the rain pours.
The same woman works at the munitions bench in the tang
  of cordite,
Bloused in hot orange. Lady, whenever your name is
  mentioned
The lawn mows itself, the french windows swing wide,
The sundials all speak the time aloud,
Rain falls in the sunshine and glitters like your blouse
In one compendious note down to my loin-bass,
I do assure you: you should hand your matches in.

IV

She makes the sign of the cross on the child's forehead
With her tongue; the Cornish logic-stone which is at times
Held uplifted by the wind; the sunset they shot
At with their arrows and the archers returned bloodstained;
The cloud-Christs blessing the hushed stone theatres;
The revenants who come close in the hope of warming
  themselves,
Out of the barrow as full of flints as leaves on a willow;
We experience the inevitable as the hard-to-gain,
But the year must change, inevitably; if we curse it,
We are bound like all cursers; the Receiver of Wrecks
Listens quietly to the teenage sonata:

He is such an old moustache.

STONED AT 'THE MEDUSA'S HEAD'

Near the sheer cliff known as *The Man and His Mother*,
Hard by the cataract called *Tall Whiteman of the West*,
I am taking a pint of luncheon at *The Medusa's Head*.
Our landlady enters, scorching her sill.
One wall of the bar-parlour is a mirror.
She will sit with me: I must swing my chair
And converse kindly through the shining wall.
She says she has gone into Undertaking,
The sign will read *Bar-Snacks and Funeral Parlour*.
She passes me the tariff, engraved on slate:
Your epitaph done in mirror-writing
On a mirror-marker so its image can read;
Your obituary illustrated with your decomposition,
Photographed monthly during your first year dead:
Full-frontal extra, to be posted in the parlour;
Widows' lockets: in the tiny silver coffin
A pinch of ashes dangling between the breasts;
Dice whittled from your shins for gambling heirs
To waste your substance with the sore dice
Of the father, 'consulting his spirit';

And her last ware: *Incorruptible Burials*,
With an item: 'hire of heavy-duty
Mortician's crane'. 'What does this mean!'
I cry, and swing round, meeting her eye,

In which I see the answer, and catch
Through the nostrils' drill-holes in my stone face
A last whiff of autumn like a smashed wine-shop.

FROM THE HOUSE UNDER THE LAKE

I

The aerial photo made of the hilltop tarn
A horned face, and of the fall that fed
The river that sped past our place,
A pillar, a fluted pillar, like a Herm
On which nature had set the shining water-head;
But at the stormy moon, the salvaged camera
From the helicopter-wreck had shown
Fed by hissing becks and ravaged by storm
A whirling medusa-head
Before the poor whirly-bird dropped like a stone.

II

A spring opened further up the hill
And took the spiral staircase to the cellar.
We let it run to carve its own features.
We have spotlights arranged to make it glitter
Like a hearth of water in the back of the house
Jigging with white flames of water-swale.
The salmon in the Spring leap our stairs.
The Captain clubs them in his net.
Those six notches in the elder-log?
To trap a poltergeist. We all make
Our living out of nature round here.
Have you tried Farmer Tissue's charged water?
It beats his cider. I carve featherlight sticks
Out of the grey lichen that feeds on the stairs.
Look at my watch: in her river-cottage workshop
Miss Cervix set this spider here.
It is hypnotised under the convex glass.
It has a perfect sense of time and points two claws
Always correctly. A third raps out the seconds.
This sliding door is where a small fly must go
At six precisely, day or night. Neglect this perk,

And it spins grey cobweb over the dial
Like a dead old lady's hair packing a locket.

ARCADY

I

The leaf scraping up the path and
Tapping at the door, ancient postman
With fresh red news.

II

A white flute, and a nudist's laugh.
The books have no covers.
The food has no plates.
The women swim like paired fish through the green groves.
A man does not hang even; is he ashamed?
My cock, my balls, love the leafy air.
Love.

III

She covered her face, power rose in her,
Juice spurted between her fingers,
I stepped towards her shouting 'Don't . . .'
But I did touch her. There was no power,
Just love turning to water,
Now it was she and I, skyclad. The great lilac tree
In the empty garden flowed as we passed it, bicycling.

IV

A boy baby, heavy as gold;
Six-pointed star, Solomon's Seal.

A baby girl, as bright as silver;
Five-pointed star, Ruler of the West.

My strength is as the strength
Of ten thousand babies.

V

The organ music, wafting along the beach!
I search for its source. An organist
In the tip-top room of this shell, or shut
In this pebble gouged by the seas,
Socketed into portals? I put
My ear-portal to it: not here
In this beetling stone, or in this pebble

Sea-pillared, or in this shell
At its proto-conch; not here:
Not a soloist at all, but everywhere:
I am the silent soloist, I must sit still.

BLIND SHIFTS

I

The great square is full of flowers I cannot see,
Only their spoors, only their scent-prints,
The heavy dabs their bright faces leave,
The spiralling air that traps the honey-bee.
There are men in this square, and women,
I believe, their odour-prints
Weave and interweave into one blanket texture,
It is the basket of a great animal called by the town's name
That creaks and smells and snaps in its own place.
These body-marks on the air, with the year's news,
The earthquakes and the letter-bombs,

Have altered, so that I am no longer sure
There are not jackals and lions trading in the city square
Among the people crying their flowers; it is like
A sudden poison-label in a cellar full of wines,
It is like the slow agaric turning away from the light
Fly-brown among the flowers that pour out like honest faces
    beaming.

II

The centipede like a strolling knot-loaf,
Or like a small dark bird's backbone running,
Or like a black monk's cloister pacing,

Or like a speeding train with windows varnished over,

Scurries, in the steel hearth, among the fir-cones.
On the mantel, black cupids clamber over a golden clock,
For love disjoints the hours: they are like
Great flies pulling a lion of days down, flies
Mightier than the lion, that consume the lion.
Among the tawny dunes, fly becomes lion.

III

After the gnawing, then the sanding in the dunes,
The smoothing and the emerying, the bone
Glassy and full of a new silence for marrow, that emptied
    bone
The ideal pillow for this dreamer, who practises
As he falls asleep, creeping out of his own ear
And entering the bone, and, like the flies of love,
Becomes the padding lion, parading through his own bone.

NAME OF ROCK OF SHELLS

The Ear penetrating the world,
The Ear everywhere, the listening
Universal spiral, the garden snail
Packs everything down to its fine point,
To its proto-conch, its little gem,
Parson's ear drills inwards
Finishes up as God, deep in his head,
The great white nebula hovers by his head
Listening; and a jest is currency,
The grim masks of God explode in smiles
To children's pretty jests; in the telescope
The spiral nebula waits for me
To tell it something that will melt
The clerical astronomer glued to its eyepiece,
He will turn and let starlight shine
Into the clockwork dome. We cut
The apple of life in two, Parson and I,
Peeled it and ate it together. To him the spiral
Nebula's thinnest point is me.
God looks over the edge, nodding,
In a gibbous hat they call a beret,
I must tell him a joke, the moon
Looking like a white bean above the rough bark
Of the tower of needles. I genuflect
To the moonlit pond, I am running the sound
Of the rain backwards and getting a fast tape
Full of voices crying plashy names abruptly
Enumerating the dead and new born; would
Parson be interested? He bends his ear; he has
An extensive theatrical wardrobe called a 'Vestry'
And reads from a certain book, dressed up in frocks
And preaches to us in the rain on Sunday, I have
Interested him in the prayers of the rain.
There is a cloudburst
And spouts from drains at the hill's foot dance
Like nude children playing in the downpour, the water

Sudsing, the conched gutter
Dressed in white ruffles for the water-party,
The cleric's black shining like a flame

Of water, and his choir drenched
Whose ruffles flop like gills, and
The whole spiralling townscape a roaring shell
Each street a stream winding to the harbour,
And full of sneezing psalms and Parson's snuffling bible.

REV. UNCLE

The cool tankard engraved in wriggle-work.
A slight scraping or nibbling noise
In the house-timbers, like boughs chafing.
The salmon-silvery river over the red rocks.
A clockwork theatre. A munumental
Calendar musical longcase bellows-clock,
That measures the lunations and strikes
Christmas again after thirteen have passed.
A salt-saw in a glass case over the fireplace.
Rev. Uncle's 'Obby 'Oss: the rotary spark discharger,
Stinking of ozone with the blue crackling spark
Leaping among its wires like a chattering monkey.
He says: 'Teeth are the most indestructible of fossils,
And I wish to understand everything to understand God,
And because it is Sunday I make electrical sparks
To remind me of His Holy Ghost, nut-cracking ape
Swinging from Apostle to Apostle chattering
In tongues. I make myself
Both literate and numerate, Peter, and the alphabet
Is God's knucklebones of Pentecost
Where he fleshes himself fingers of flame, my lover,
And in algebra numbers are letters, you can hear
God's voice of creation when you vibrate the equations . . .'
And he did so, singing quadratics,

130

'Let X be middle C: now strike me an A . . .'
And I did so, on the piano.
'Not that the fossil-stone is a shut-in god,
Say rather it is a constant, something so slow
It shows its godlikeness only by residence
In many centuries. Don't tell the Bishop
But God-Mumgod made the world in their image;
Virgins like you will understand in due time . . .
Ma-God is a sea-maid, created from brine
Delicate skinned patterns of beating gonads
Like a fleet of umbrellas frailer than rain
Each like a seawater castle or mandala
A curtained pulse of bliss of the sea
And I tell you, boy, being dead is like that,
A celestial jellyfish shaped like the sky, beating, beating,
A whole eye, grazing on aether . . . but I love
Being God's vicar on two legs, lad, and the hymns,
Give me that A again . . .'

In my Uncle's library, my Mother's brother,
Every book and stone after church
Speaking his tongue, and on the brass lamp
His dog-collar swinging like a starched half-moon.

GIRL OUT OF EGYPT

The nettle, red fire up to the elbow,
Green fire in the undergrowth.
I will give her that valley for a door of hope.
Blood touches blood, in the lip-bleb.
We are sooth and soothed in meditation, at last.

In the solar room the strong hot beams
Cross and recross from glass to glass,
A strong pressure of breeze arises, it whispers

131

Behind closed doors through the house.
They had done more than this, to set up

Eternal winds speaking oracles in sealed pyramids:
It is told they fed wild beasts with manflesh
Until beast spoke to beast through clotted teeth;

And all other races to them wore the down
Of juvenility on their souls, like the Greeks.

THE LARYNX IN THE HILL

A blazing glass head has risen up out of the well
Pulling the brickwork after it; there! the lighthouse
Shines again, just beyond

A row of cottage whorehouses, brightly-lit

Where the waterfall leans back like a figure sighing
Throned on fat cushions of water, with hands
Of water and white nails scoring the weir
By a row of bollards worn into smooth smiles
By towing-ropes, and a mill-wheel that is black
Scooping white spadefuls of water; a larynx

Made of brick, slate, mica, timber and
A quantity of water falling
In one note of sigh;

The people seldom speak, even in bed,
The water falling is the village word,
Its only name, its surname, the white sound of everything.

LILITH, LAZARUS AND THE ANGEL

I

God, the cherubim-maker,
Enthroned on his cherubim-machinery;

Hide the light and it makes the husks,
Hidden light makes living moulds;

Lilith wrapped in living velvet.

This is the secret of the children's smiling
It is because of Lilith who plays with them when they are
    small,
Life cannot match it, they are wrapped in living velvet again,

They recall it, seek it.

It may be there at their latter end,
Death wrapped in living velvet.
They may return to Her, almost before leaving Her,
Called back into the living velvet.

II

The angel with the silken lungs,
The white, perfectly-clean air-sacs
Collapsed except when annunciating,
Or chorusing Christmas;
And the folded bowels
Like a drawer-full of ironed hankies,
Kept for table-manners with human folk.
Lazarus is at table too,
He receives asides by thought-transference:

His brains are neatly folded-away like linens,
He does not need them, he is full of knowledge,

Like the knowledge of the dew that comes down
Through the caverns of the sky after a hard day

And lies with a calm stare over all grass

This is Lazarus' stare as he sits at table
Opposite me, with no conversation,
But a smile I am glad to see,
And under his skin death
Like a freshly pressed wardrobe of clothes,
With one angel and me for company,

Like white evening dress
And pink decorations worn like pale roses in the cheeks

A little too clean, and a little too sharply pressed;
Not quite a gentleman he jokes about his first death.

TANTRIC RITES

I

Moonlight wrapped into a labyrinth,
Wrapped into a shoal of fish, woven
Out of the water, the tidal floods,

Landed on an upturned bucket
During a seamen's strike, and fishermen,

Dammit, are selling the fish themselves,
Without middlemen, or giving the fish away,
As a demonstration, the silvery sea-mice
That run through the corridors of tide,
The water-brooches of the moon,

'Make a nice change from chicken, Mum',

The labyrinthine.

II

The youth wore a garnet ring
Carved into a cock and balls;
He told us all a cock-and-ball story,

A story of seduction and salvation,
Of love, of tantric love,

The skin
Breaking out in eyes, all over, blinking
In rhythmic waves, so at no time
Was any of the skin blind,
The lids opening, closing

As a breeze travels over the field of tall wheat
That springs out of the black mud,

The field feels it, as the rootlets tug,
Retina-carpet, the field sees it,
Weather, breeze and earthquake visible,

Swore the youth with his flesh and blood in the bottomless
    vessel
Of garnet carved into cock and balls.

III

After the entertainments are over,
The masks are allowed to rot;

He dresses in masks that reach to his knees,
A beaded skirt, and an auburn scalp-mask
Luxuriant and burning, and a flexible face-mask
Of breath-taking pigments, for he

Feeling holy, went to his death in splendid drag,

Children clothed in silver-foil and acute snouts
Masked like silvery well-mice, followed him dancing,
Were not permitted to see his masks bleed
And emptied out into the grave, or his death-face scrubbed.

INAQUATION

The cold bars of the fountain; he was encaged
And it ran corrupt for sixty days, and then
Had washed all flesh off the bone; after a hundred weeks
The skeleton hairy-green with weed-locks
Inhumed; maybe the man's son ready to be water-caged
In his father's place. If any did die while the
Only fountain ran corrupt with the beetle-coloured
    waters
And hummed deep *Om* with flies (thick as blackberries
On the water-bush) he was salted down
To wait his turn, slow queue. In the great plague,
Masons, recovered and immune, constructed plentifully
Sufficient fountains equipped with dead-thrones,
But now the practice has by law been discontinued, all
    fountains
Run clean and pure over our fathers' feathering bones.

SEVERAL KINDS OF SYLLABLE

I

The oak in the wind cries like a living baby.
Whose cradle will I cut out of its wood?

The wind springs through, bowing all its twigs
Like a violin which has three thousand strings.

All possible utterances in those oak-cries,
Birth-music, death-hums, love-cries:
I will carve a set of cradle-cries out of that wood.

The tree carves bright dusty paths
Out of sunlight, like corridors
Opening and shutting, it plaits
A globe of web over the sun
That shuttles light,
Shuttles dark,
Like legs, like arms, crossing, uncrossing.

II

If it creeps across your path,
Break the stick of the seedling oak.
Chew the infant wood, it gives a little honey.
The hairy head of the sun in the oak
Climbs out naked over the roof

Turning to gold my accountant's house
Who as a yachtsman knowing the tides
And the financial structure of the planet
Keeps an ironic distance in his manner
Which is a fiscal secret,
And can fix a stopped car.

In front of the accountant's house
The oak stands like a great official,
A universal sundial, moondial,
An uncountable being, whose slow syllables are audible
In stilled chatter. The raindrops
In celestial multitudes snake down the stems,

Round the light in each soft lens and shatter it;

It is all part of the first syllable; hush!
Here comes the second, made of thousands
Of bright rained eyes, uncalculated.

DUST DOES NOT SLEEP

Where is there any dust!

I travel up the corridors of the bird's voice,
There is a green meadow off the glacier,
There is a moth in the skull (all that's left of him)
A glow-worm in the skull; in the next-door tomb
A skeleton sits with firefly studs.
The seamoths flutter above the wave-crests;
The little spiders: the looms with eyes;
The water-castle in the tin cup, the trembling
Pier-glasses and curved corridors;

                              how the dry
Pillow drinks from me, how the parched feathers
Of the rain-birds drink from me!

THREE-HUNDRED-YEAR MOMENT
(*For G.M.*)

See the skeleton
And thou seest Death;
See the interior of the skeleton
And thou seest the Awakener.
The smoke motionless over the bonfire,
Cerebral enfilades; the fire has stopped to watch itself:

The beetle on the consuming leaf
Continues feeding
Among the stiff, hindered flames.
Who can tell
When the smoke
Will begin rolling again
When the flames
Will leap into their fiddle again, and eat?
Now they are like coiled shells,
Rosy with light, with fringes
A little stained with grey, like a cluster
Of shells of yellow and purple
Tied with ribbons of smoke;

I am a bouquet, says the fire,
With a grey hood, like a monk,
At this speed — but I am

At my fastest a bomb-blast,
And I am everywhere, in fact, says the fire,
This pile of leaves or that candle or that filament
Make me visible, that is all,

Let the bouquet live dangerously fast,
I mean the one in her hand, and she loses
The hand in a flash; let the grass
Live at the speed the sun burns
And we are dead in an instant;

And the trees, the grey volutes
Lope away over the red-hot fence,

Or stand for a three-hundred-year moment.

DISGUST, PASSING

I have a hot sweater knitted of dog's-wool,
My rectum rejects a pungent brown spectre,
I pull a glue-ghost from a deep black nostril;
The clouds will not rain, they glow
In pulses like the TV broken down,

A fine pearl like the gaunt leaves of nettles,
Their silky phantasmal hair full of acid,
Closed with a stopple of flint so tiny
It would not trouble an eye

These silky gauntlets
Are green ghosts out of these graves full of death-stings

The wind a wending web, the wind a bending diamond,

An old ghost slides out of brickwork in its apple-suit

I touch one of its apples, rough as brick to my hand,
I pluck it, and eat stone-flesh, full of cider-spirit.

TEMPTATION OF THE BOOKS

I

The skull-like walnut, the hazel like a combed head.
Dreams of the past wasted like sand. An Aztec calendar

Which is like a compass, which is like a shrine
Which is a navigational instrument

The sun with his tongue out in the centre of it.

And I saw a little thing the size of a nut
In God's palm, 'It is all that is made', he said:

It was his shrine-clock he had pulled out of his fob,
Or his acorn full of oak-forests where we evolved,
Or his ovary which is a menstrual timepiece,
Or a fistful of ore full of metal fighting
To get out on the roads and eat petrol
Or a lump of Germanium
Of the quality required to pick up a colour transmission.

An eye looks at me from the bottom of my cup,
I put it there, it is made with mirror,
I drink, and my cup looks back at me.

II

The Doubting Thomas Divining Set:
A pregnant woman. The baby in its water leaps in her
Who passes over aquastats, or by tumuli

Where these hidden springs of water are mistaken for ghosts
With their snaky locks and their misty wings
Rising and filing between the trunks; these are the upper
    shapes
Of streams flitting between the forested roots;
Let a pregnant woman divine them.

III

They pierced his ears so that he could understand
The letters within his head. The dead man's shirt
Worn very tight buttoned to the throat.
The corpse lying within the soiltide
Under the airtide by the tidal sea:
In the long black boats
Under the slate figure-heads,
Under the moon, they float away.

141

IV

Under the moon made of granite
Definite and hard as a dead man's shirt.
Jupiter's Callisto is a pumice like a bath-stone,
Would float on our brine sea, riding high;
Mars' Deimos
Is not so great as our Mount Everest;
Phobos of Mars rises in the West, like witches
Spinning withershins:

The whole solar system,
The long-body of the sun, is made of rings
Like a great tree of spinning orbits;

They say that human thoughts
Are stored in brain-atom orbits;
Thoughts of thoughts
Stored in the moons' erratic orbits;

Including the snowball Jupiter moons;
Enough memory

Stored in the moons to waken the dead.

V

Wine made of the dead whose carcasses fatten the soil:

Thus is a man beside himself when he has drunk,
For he is filled with the blood of his ancestors;
Everything photographed into the blood;
He dies, his photographs draining into the soil;

The planets are god's bones, his flesh their motions,

Everything photographed by starlight;

Her nightgown exchanges with the sheets,
She goes to bed in red, she rises in white,
The books of the shelves babbling like wooden bells.

VI

An obstetrics which is a cosmogony.
Some had drunk a thing which froze the heart
And left nothing but a love of dancing.

He wears his guilt like a neat black suit.

The lady is a toad, green and well turned-out;
Seven had their wedding with the ropemaker's daughter
And are learning to fly. He passes twelve
Black dogs on smouldering chains, to set the house free.
I am like an ant caught in the folds of her skirt,

And this is how the earth's story changes, as she turns
I run, or the green plains unfold
And I build my generations, then
The woman turns again and I am hunted
Like the ant on a green skirt, like the spider

Swinging into nothing on plaited sinews.

LIGHT HOTEL

The little girl riding the fallen tree like a spindly horse,
Like a queen mounted on a green spider;
The little girl's white flesh is so sacred, so queenly,
I love and fear it so much

Carefully I think only of her dress,
Her foliate dress that falls in dry green pleats,
Or think as I look away from her sunlit face

143

How the sunlight holds a great conference in a sandgrain
With its plate-glass terraces and vista-windows of gold-tinge,

Then how the moon will hold her conference in the same
    sealed chamber.
In between times the non-staff have no clearing to do, no
    ashes to empty,
No glasses to polish, the light simply passes, great guest,

The light simply passes from the hotel, it is left untouched,
And above the million sand-grains, the one girl swishing her
    wide green horse.

MYSTERY STORY

I

He offers us blank coins
We are to pay for our initiations with blank coins
They are round fragments of mirror
The superscription a puzzled sky
With your face looking down out of it
Or your fingers turning the mirror
Till your eye flashes out of it;
We are shown a garden,
The growth of it is the growth of the divine substance,
There is an effigy in privet of a hanged man
He is sprouting with beady flowers,
They are like his whitehard fats,
They spring out of what they depict;

Mud is moulded with spices to an image of the Moon
Which is then robed gorgeously,
A glass of water is drunk, to the shout 'Osiris is found!'
We are to keep our coins
I use mine to see to trim my beard

144

Are they laughing behind their baby-faces at us?
Is it priestcraft, are they lying, am I Osiris?

II

The backbone is at Busiris
Isis fanned the cold clay with her wings
Everywoman does this, as her winged womb waxes
There was a lake at Sais, on which the sufferings were
    displayed
On lighted boats, at night;

His backbone: everywhere, like the roads of houses,
The feathery willow-walk, the Orion stars;

I have gathered him inside me, I have eaten earth,
It conforms to me, the clay grows warm.

III

In a broad urn that is fluted like a clam
A tall fountain stands dressed as a bride
Who bobs and falters, shuffles, who has white hair
That veils her. The fountains, like flowers,
Have roots in the mountains, roots in the clouds,
The tree of life which is water has flowers in the ocean,
Roots in the sky. He spends an hour on his side
Watching the wedding of streams, the conchoidal responses,
An hour on his back watching
The roots of water writhe over the moon,
Cockroach-colours, or in the sunshine
White as potato-rootlets, rootlets of fat rivers.
Thunder licks the mountain as a sign of assemblage.
Sky-clambering rivers shadow the hoary battlefield.

THE WORK

I

Give me the cliff glasses. Look at the pine orchard
Of fir apples. There is a pond barrow
Almost silted with bones. In that cave
The shadows are so ancient they are frozen
Like engravings to the wall, layer on layer.
Hand me the shadow-acid, we must clean this cave,
The sooty old ones are thick enough to whisper, now,
But we must get on with living. No, your friend
Will not be scrubbed. She is not old enough
In death to walk about without bones,
Not detached enough from putrefaction
For fit society. One day you shall meet her
Under the night city, slice of the star-pomegranate.

II

The green-doctors with their mirrors of red gold.
A root which does the bidding of its owner:
The sleepy root, one dreams it is a friend:
There is someone there who communicates from the earth
In sips of hot root tea from underground
By the tidal estuary, which slides its shining bolts,
Raising its hands of mud as the moon passes.
The green doctors, affronted by the naked shine,
Sew a cloth map for her funeral pall
To fling over the long black glassy coffin
So it seems a country they are burying:
Corduroy tacked in ploughed fields, the city stitched
In strict serge and woollen pinstripe, the woods and hills
Of tweed, a satin river sewn to a silken sea.

III

Over to the south the city lay in streets
Like glowworms on a bush, like the stars

146

Hovering between electricities. Hearse hooves
Clattered across laboratory concrete.
Glass tubes pulse with glowworms, a bench
Is fitted and flasked with the phosphorescent work.
Hares run in the cyclotrons, spiders count the scintilla
Like electrical dew strung in cloud-chambers;
Galvanometers, as the sides of the silvery chilled horse,
   twitch.

IV

Embalmed in a coffin packed with ivy-leaves,
Nice and musty, just an old skull
And a few dry toffee-strings, very small boneface
With thin sticks among the admirable ivy-must
Like that which coats old houses crumbling to dust,
Houses that have lost their persons,
Bodies that have lost their persons.
This house has ivy curtains, this dead girl
Eyelids of ivy, all over her.

V

The embalmer packed her mouth and vagina
With fresh rose-leaves when the prostitute died;
Her dress was a soft machinery of glimpses;
Suddenly all the stones in the mountains,
All the beach pebbles corrupted like spoiled fruit;
The frost-birds perched in the bracken.
She came back to me in the form
Of her deeply-resourceful perfume full of many recesses
Though the chief of these would never return
That had never done less than chirp, most often
Would crow and flap its wings for I went so deep
Into her the weather improved for a week, in her
By her permission, my soul attained womanhood.

147

ENCOUNTERS

I

Two gods slaying the storm
Represented by a lion with a raining mane,

Or by a goddess, holding a great mirror
And wearing a necklace of mirrors,

I saw her, she started up,
Stood like wires burning in the cloud's mouth
Roaring with its manes opening into mouths
That opened roaring.

II

The scenery of a feast:
The light, the white shirts
White like clothes of light,
The skin, opening its lattices and billowing,
Opening its throats to the sunshine.
And what did that? Innumerable caresses
Spelling out the afternoon
Among light linens in a high wide bed,
Does this not open to the light within?

Can you not see how it billows, the skin,
Like a pulsing draught in a flourmill,
Like the flanks of a white bull,

Like a sudden growth of eider all over me?
Can't you? Then he will wear his loose shirt,
And I will wear a lace dress all of loose knots,

The whiteness and the billowing will show
We have stepped through the white mirror together
And back again — look at this, the reflections are loosening,

There are rising under the oldskins, relenting new ones.

III

The louse found on clean linen:
Sickness in the family, death;
The Thinkers in Things, and the Predictors;
The Thinkers in insects, birds, tides,
In moon-phases and trees, sleep.
Sex, and then such deep sleep,
Incubating our syrups for many hours,

Dreaming of Ox-chapels within,
Bison sanctuaries, and Bison chapels
Within Ox cathedrals, how handsome
The great cathedrals of the beasts
Painted into glass windows and crowned with blood-roses!

IV

A snake-headed lion on a gallows.
The small boy shows what a big water-penis he has.
A Spenser with a design of gods and prisoners.
Sea-shells that resemble snake-skulls, were mistaken for them.
A chalice-fragment with a marsh-scene.
A sceptre inscribed with a New Year's greeting.

Seashells like snakeskulls coming in with hisses
On the snaky water-bodies of the tide,

The great wave that follows the Moon, face-upward,

The wave full of water-faces and white manes,
The great mane-headed herd or world-traveller
Who roars soft or loud all round the world
With manes settling into eyes that open on eyes

Reading upward from his streaked hood the irregular
    moonscript.

TALL HAIRDO

I

Her bronze hair beaten into a bearded face looking backwards,
She posed for her photo by the orchard, her coiffure
Stared backwards deep into the blossom where the clear
   stream raced
Full of its rippling fishes without blood, bones or skin
That wait for the apples to drop and become cider in them.
Open the wooden doors! cried that face
As her backwards-countenance stared deep into the trees.
I took my photo to purify the air,
Memory will perfect itself with its aid

Like bees sipping honey from a picture,
Painted flowers, real honey.

II

That face!
The grass grows fast in the starlight,
The sheep's entrails smell of mown grass and starlight,
The dew falls on the grass like the stars descending to feast;
That bronze gaze does it!
The rich bodies of stars
Covered with molten syrups and roasting waxes
Have dark-distilled themselves into featherings of moisture.

III

Remembering Jupiter's shadow
Peering out of the bronze hair-do,
In the roasting sun I smash that black
Bristling Devon fly: popping out of its back
Fat bunches of sallow eggs across the thin green window,
Like a banana-truck packed with yellow bananas in vehicular
   black,
Like smashing a flying ear of wheat which is black.

IV

The grave countenance of polished hair
Climbs into the evening;
There are clouds like Buddhas of slithering flour,
There are Butter-Buddhas of fatness, sunset-melting,
There are Buddhas of flowing pearly wax,
And now the storm, of great black-eyed Buddhas
Thrusting quick enlightenment from goffered halls.
Morning Buddhas climb rungs of frill and ruff, in the quiet air
White gulls turn, fine themselves
To a razor-line, turn back
A countenance alighting with a lemon stare,
A hooked nose, adjusting feather garments round a look
Rustling, of gold and black like apple-bees,

A waspish eye with a centre
Like the cold black earth flying a sunshine corridor.

V

She looks out of the picture,
Her bronze countenance facing backwards
Pores over the gravestones at St Materiana's:
Smooth bald slate to the east, light lichen coastwards.
We paced it out
Like walking through a great black tree
Of silver-lined leaves, changing as we passed
The colour of God's acre.

VI

The croaking frogs in the springtime:
The cries of unborn children.
The light shower sets the wood ticking
Like a great oval watch made of many oval drops.
For modesty, she looks down at her feet;
The bronze face rears up, alert:

Suddenly all the hoar oaks are chattering with auburn sunlight
As though troops of monkeys with torches ran through the
boughs.

VII

Your inward skin studded with eyes like yonis
Looking down within you like the stars
Dilating out of blackness: there presides
Your photo-face and a bronze countenance watching
backwards.
All the stars are gliding to fresh places,
Fretting as they glide, twirling like gimlets.
As they pass over, the dark apple-trees
Release their perfume in slow explosions.
They relimn into a new constellation
With two profiles that is the whole sky.

The moon climbs its slow hill to the centre,
Wish! it hangs there like a mirror.
Then the sun rises and does not put the stars out:
They shine still, strong black rays, and beams of perfume.

HAPPINESS

A great lamp with a secret room;
A cathedral built under a waterfall;
A haunted wig placed on the polished piano.

Whitemetal cufflinks stamped with a profile of Lucifer;
The stewpot full of springwater, a diet of wild seeds,
The lake waxing and waning, brimming with bogbean,
Nettles and waterlily, meadowed with salads;
A tame gazelle and an ever-full inkpot;
A stain on my shirt over the heart where the milk runs;
The superb ceremonial cape from Mold.

The hellish breath of the bounding bell-metal
Calling good folk to meeting, red-hot with ringing;
A house with a black wall, in the garden an oak
Recording in wooden graph-lines three hundred weather-
    years;

Courses of old bricks, like unity almost appearing;
A thousand sheep, that roam the dewy mountain;
A case of needles winking eyes in the firelight;
A flower heavy with itself, still as sandstone;

Honky-tonk on the wooden harp at a picnic in Beef Park,
My song in a sealskin waistcoat and a soft white shirt.